本书为广东省哲学社会科学规划项目"《论语》翻译叙事的多模态建构研究"（GD22CWY01）及广东省高等教育教学研究和改革项目"基于《理解当代中国》的财经院校英语类专业课程体系教学改革与实践"的研究成果

《论语》英译赏析

Appreciating English Translations of *The Analects*

胡红辉◎编著

中山大学出版社
SUN YAT-SEN UNIVERSITY PRESS

·广州·

图书在版编目（CIP）数据

《论语》英译赏析/胡红辉编著 . —广州：中山大学出版社，2022. 12
ISBN 978 - 7 - 306 - 07791 - 2

Ⅰ. ①论…　Ⅱ. ①胡…　Ⅲ. ①《论语》—英语—翻译—研究　Ⅳ. ①H315. 9
②B222. 25

中国国家版本馆 CIP 数据核字（2023）第 089248 号

出 版 人：王天琪
策划编辑：熊锡源
责任编辑：熊锡源
封面设计：林绵华
责任校对：李昭莹
责任技编：靳晓虹
出版发行：中山大学出版社
电　　话：编辑部 020 - 84110771，84110283，84111997，84110779
　　　　　发行部 020 - 84111998，84111981，84111160
地　　址：广州市新港西路 135 号
邮　　编：510275　传　　真：020 - 84036565
网　　址：http://www.zsup.com.cn　E-mail：zdcbs@ mail. sysu. edu. cn
印 刷 者：佛山市浩文彩色印刷有限公司
规　　格：787mm×1092mm　1/16　7.5 印张　165 千字
版次印次：2022 年 12 月第 1 版　2022 年 12 月第 1 次印刷
定　　价：30. 00 元

前　言

　　《论语》是中国文化经典之作，为"五经之辖辖，六艺之喉衿"，是研究孔子及儒家思想的第一手资料，在世界文明中享有广泛的声誉，产生了深远的影响，其英译本也层出不穷，翻译者和评论家已形成"译介＋评述"的循环助推模式，相关译介研究亦呈攀升态势，爆发之期可待。

　　本书是以国内外现存的知名英译本为语料，适合本科院校英语类专业学生及对中国经典著作英译感兴趣的非英语类专业本科生使用的中国经典著作英译赏析教材。

　　本书认为对原文思想及核心概念的正确理解为《论语》英译难点，针对英语类专业学生的现状和未来发展需要，聚焦正确诠释源语问题以丰富和提高英语类专业学生的汉语知识和应用能力；同时，通过对《论语》不同章节、不同英译本的赏析与评价，反复品阅比对典籍原文与译文，仔细考究文体变异与结构重选，剖析贯穿《论语》各英译文的叙述暗流，明晰显性叙事与隐形叙事的双轨进程，描绘典籍译本叙事表意路径，提高学生分析问题、解决问题的能力，提高学生的人文素养，全面提高学生的综合素质。

　　本书共分七章。第一章对《论语》英译做一个简要的介绍，包括现存的主要英译本、《论语》英译的主要难点和重点等；第二章通过具体的实例，探讨《论语》原文与英文在句法结构上的相似之处及主要差异，以及《论语》英译中通常采取的翻译策略和技巧；第三章至第七章通过具体的实例，赏析不同译者对于《论语》中关于"学""仁""孝""君子""君子与小人"等不同主题的论述的英文译文，探讨不同译者对于《论语》原文中所表达思想的不同解释与翻译。每章都附有练习，旨在使学生熟悉和巩固该章所学的重要内容。各章的练习均有参考答案，集中附于书末。本书的《论语》现代汉语译文分别来自杨伯峻（2006）、李泽厚（2004）、钱穆（2011）、天宜（2010），所选英文译文分别来自理雅各、辜鸿铭、许渊冲及吴国珍的英译版本，在书中均有注明。书末附上理雅各所译《论语》一至十篇英译文，供读者参考阅读。

　　本书可用作一个学期的课程教材，每周两节，可视学生的实际程度而定。鉴于笔者的能力与知识水平有限，本书在设计与编写中不可避免地存在不足与缺陷，有待广大教师和学生在使用过程中帮助我们不断完善，使其更好地服务于我国英语类专业本科教学工作及学科建设与翻译人才的培养，以及高等院校非英语类本科生的通识人才培养。

目　　录

第一章 《论语》英译概述

《论语》作为中国典籍的代表作品，迄今已有超过 60 种英译本，但是新的译本依然不断出现。本章主要介绍《论语》在对外传播的过程中产生的主要译本和主要特征，以及《论语》英译的难点。

一、《论语》的主要英译版本

按照出版时间的先后顺序，这里简单列举以下 27 种《论语》的主要英译本。

1. Marshman，J. 1809. *The Works of Confucius：Containing the Original Text，with a Translation.* Vol. 1：1 – 725. Serampore：the Mission Press.

Marshman（1809）通常被认为是《论语》英译的开山之作，但该译本仅含《论语》的前十篇，即《论语》的"上论"部分（吴国向，2013：167）。

2. Collie，D. 1828. *The Chinese Classical Works Commonly Called the Four Books.* Malacca：the Mission Press.

Collie（1828）翻译的这部"四书"包括"前言"、"孔子传记"、《大学》译本、《中庸》译本、《论语》译本、"孟子传记"和《孟子》译本等。《论语》译本为全译本，即包含《论语》"上论"和"下论"两部分（吴国向，2013：168）。

3. Legge，J. 1861. *The Chinese Classics：With a Translation，Critical and Exegetical Notes，Prolegomena，and Copious Indexes.* Vol. 1. London：Trübuner&co.

作为新教传教士、汉学家和牛津大学第一任汉学教授，理雅各（James Legge）对中国古代经典的翻译与诠释做出了巨大贡献（姜哲，2015：34）。他的《论语》翻译讲究译文对原文的忠实。1893 年，这部著作经过理雅各的修订，实现再版。他翻译的主要参考依据是朱熹的《集注》。

4. Wade，T. F. 1869. *The Lun Yü：Being Utterances of Kung Tzu，Known to the Western World as Confucius.* Herford：S. Austin.

这个译本的译者韦妥玛，是韦氏拼音系统（Wade-Giles System）的创始人之一。这个拼音系统至今依然应用于《论语》的英语翻译。

5. Jennings，W. 1895. *The Confucian Analects：A Translation with Annotation and Introduction.* London：George Routledge and Sons.

詹宁斯的译本标题为《儒家论语：翻译附加注解与介绍》，是《论语》的全译本。

6. Ku, H. M. （辜鸿铭）1898. *The Discourses and Sayings of Confucius：A New Special Translation，Illustrated with Quotations from Goethe and Other Writers*. Shanghai：Kelly and Walsh.

辜鸿铭是第一个将《论语》翻译成英文的中国人，他精通中、英两种语言，觉得西方传教士的翻译没有完全表达《论语》的本义，所以决定自己翻译《论语》。

7. Giles, L. 1907. *The Sayings of Confucius：A New Translation of the Greater Part of the Confucian Analects*. London：John Murray.

这部译本的译者是韦氏拼音系统的改良者和推广人。此译本是《论语》原文大部分内容的翻译，不是全译本。

8. Soothill, W. E. 1910. *The Analects of Confucius*. Edinburgh：Oliphant, Anderson & Ferrier.

这部全译本，除了主体的翻译部分，还包括简要的中国古代年鉴、孔子的 36 位弟子的简介、注释和人物列表等（吴国向，2013：169）。

9. Lin, Y. T. （林语堂）1938. *The Wisdom of Confucius*. New York：The Modern Library.

这部《孔子的智慧》由林语堂完成出版，里面包含"孔子的格言《论语》"一章。林语堂从十个方面对孔子加以解读，并且从《论语》中选择相应的语句加以翻译，并非《论语》的全译本（吴国向，2013：169）。

10. Waley, A. 1938. *The Analects of Confucius*. London：G. Allen & Unwin Ltd.

亚瑟·威利翻译的是《论语》全本。除了正文的英语翻译，译本还包括前言、引论、注释、附录和索引等。其中，引论部分介绍了中国远古和先秦时期的重要历史人物、孔子弟子、《论语》本身、关键术语、文言传统和礼仪等。威利自己对此译本的评论是：翻译不是文学翻译，而是技术翻译，因此缺乏文学风味（吴国向，2013：170）。

11. Hughes, E. R. 1942. *Chinese Philosophy in Classical Times*. London：J. M. Dent & Sons/New York：E. P. Button & Co. Inc.

《中国古代哲学》这本书包含《论语》的部分翻译。译者采用的研究视角是哲学的，可以算作现代时期较早采取哲学角度审视《论语》的著作（吴国向，2013：170）。

12. Pound, E. 1969. *Confucius：The Great Digest, the Unwobbling Pivot, the Analects*. New York：New Directions.

庞德翻译的这本《孔子：大学、中庸、论语》包含《论语》的翻译。庞德受到儒家道德和政治学说的影响，曾经大量翻译中国典籍。

13. Ware, J. R. 1955. *The Sayings of Confucius*. New York：New American Library.

这本《孔子语录》是译者针对西方大众读者的全译本（吴国向，2013：170）。

14. Faucett, L. 1978. *The Sayings of Confucius：A New Translation of the Analects Based Closely on the Meaning and Frequency of the Characters*. San Diego：Faucett.

译者1922年来华，身负宗教使命，入驻苏州大学，通过语言教学、语言研究和教材编写等方式影响中国（吴国向，2013：171）。

15. Lau, D. C.（刘殿爵）1979. *The Analects（Lun Yü）*. New York：Penguin Books.

刘殿爵的这本译作是全译本。

16. Zhang, W. L.（张威麟）1985.《中、英、西、葡对照〈论语〉》。香港：孔子学出版社。

张威麟的这部译作作为全译本，提供中、英、西、葡四语对照。

17. Dawson, R. 1993. *The Analects*. Oxford：Oxford University Press.

Dawson的这部译本，定位为儒学入门读本，面向不具备中国语言和哲学传统知识的读者群体（吴国向，2013：173）。

18. Tsai，C. C.（蔡志忠）and Bruya. B. 1996. *Confucius Speaks：Words to Live By*. New York：Anchor Books.

此书为《论语》漫画选译本，蔡志忠负责漫画创作，Bruya负责翻译创作。

19. Huang, C. C.（黄继忠）1997. *The Analects of Confucius：A Literal Translation with an Introduction and Notes*. New York：Oxford University Press.

黄继忠于1983年受邀至美国讲授《论语》，在此后近20年去国怀乡的日子里，黄继忠相继翻译了《论语》《道德经》等中文典籍。基于海外华人译者共有的离散经历，黄继忠译本呈现出华人译者译本的共性因子。透过其《论语》英译本，可以看到译者的文化身份对译本形成的影响，以及作为华人译者的黄继忠在其译本中坚持选择直译翻译策略的原因（屠国元、许雷，2013）。

20. Leys，S. 1997. *The Analects of Confucius*. New York：W. W. Norton & Company.

译者在该译本的序言里指出，译本面向的读者不是同行学者，而是大众读者，主要包括那些无法直接从原文获取知识却希望扩展自身文化视野的广大人士（吴国向，2013：174）。

21. Wang, F. L.（王福林）1997.《〈论语〉详注及英译》。上海：世界图书出版公司。

22. Ames, R. T. and H. Rosemont, Jr. 1998. *The Analects of Confucius：A Philosophical Translation*. New York：Ballantine Pub. Group.

这是一部从哲学的角度进行阐释的《论语》英译本。

23. Brooks, E. B. and A. T. Brooks. 1998. *Original Analects：Sayings of Confucius and His Successor*. New York：Columbia University Press.

此译本放弃了原文的篇章结构安排，按照译者研究所得出的《论语》语句形成先后顺序重新编排和翻译。

24. Slingerland, E. G. 2003. *Confucius Analects：with Selection from Traditional Commentaries*. Indianapolis：Hackett Publishing Company.

译者在译本里指出，其译本的目标读者为非专业人士。

25. Xu, Y. C.（许渊冲）2005. *Confucius Modernized，Thus Spoke the Master*. Beijing：Higher Education Press.

许渊冲在翻译中强调创造性，强调《论语》的现代化解读。

26. Song, D. L.（宋德利）2010.《〈论语〉英汉对照》，北京：对外经济贸易大学出版社。

27. Wu, G. G.（吴国珍）2012. *A New Annotated English Version of the Analects of Confucius*. Fuzhou：Fujian Education Press.

中国学者吴国珍的译本，也是近十多年来的《论语》新译本。

二、《论语》英译的难点

典籍英译者不但要通晓中国语言和文化，特别是汉语文言和中国古典文学，而且要精通英语和西方文化。只有这样，他们才能对原著融会贯通，翻译时才能将原文的微妙之处传递出来，运用译文语言才能游刃有余。《论语》英译的难点，不仅仅体现在英文表达之难，还体现在理解原文之难。

（一）《论语》原文中"名"与"字"的区分

在古代，由于特别重视礼仪，所以关于"名""字"的称呼是十分讲究的。在人际交往中，"名"一般用作谦称、卑称，或上对下、长对少的称呼，"名"是幼时取的，供长辈呼唤。平辈之间，只有在很熟悉的情况下才相互称"名"，在多数情况下，提到对方或他人时直呼其"名"，被认为是一种不礼貌的行为。平辈之间，相互称"字"，则被认为是有礼貌的表现。"字"往往是"名"的解释和补充，是与"名"相表里的，所以又称"表字"。男子到了二十岁成年，要举行冠礼，这标志着本人要出仕，进入社会。女子长大后也要离开母家而许嫁，未许嫁的叫"未字"，亦可叫"待字"。待十五岁许嫁时，举行笄礼，也要取"字"，供朋友呼唤。下对上、卑对尊写信或呼唤时，可以称对方的"字"，但绝对不能称其"名"，尤其是君主或自己父母长辈的"名"，更是连提都不能提，否则便是"大不敬"或叫"大逆不道"。

译者如未能正确理解中文古文中"名"与"字"的区别，就有可能造成《论语》原文语篇中提到的人名的误译。现将《论语》所涉及的孔子主要弟子的姓、名及字分别列举如下：颜回（姓颜，名回，字子渊）；冉耕（姓冉，名耕，字伯牛）；冉雍（姓冉，名雍，字仲弓）；冉求（姓冉，名求，字子有）；仲由（姓仲，名由，字子路）；宰予（姓宰，名予，字子我）；端木赐（姓端木，名赐，字子贡）；颜偃（姓颜，名偃，字子游）；卜商（姓卜，名商，字子夏）；曾参（姓曾，名参，字子舆）；澹台灭明（姓澹台，名灭明，字子羽）；宓不齐（姓宓，名不齐，字子贱）；公冶长（姓公冶，名长，字子长）；司马耕（姓司马，名耕，字子牛）；漆雕开（姓漆雕，名开，字子开）；公西赤（姓公西，名赤，字子华）；有若（姓有，名若，字子有）；冉季（姓冉，名季，字子产）。

《论语》原文第一篇第十五章，为子贡与孔子的一段对话。"子贡"是孔子弟子"端木赐"的"字"，"赐"其"名"。《论语》由孔子的弟子及再传弟子编撰而成，编撰者可能为子贡的平辈或后辈，因而原文用"子贡"这个"字"来指称"端木赐"；而在对话中，孔子为端木赐的老师，因而直接用其名"赐"来称呼他，如下文所示：

子贡曰："贫而无谄，富而无骄，何如？"子曰："可也；未若贫而乐，富而好礼者也。"

子贡曰："诗云：'如切如磋，如琢如磨'，其斯之谓与？"子曰："赐也，始可与言诗已矣，告诸往而知来者。"（《论语》1/15）①

在英文译文中，有些译者在充分理解原文"名"与"字"之间区别的基础上，通过对"名"和"字"的不同翻译，在译文中体现其差异；有些译者选择用同样的词翻译原文中的"名"和"字"，未能体现原文中"名"与"字"的差别，因而造成译文在人称意义上与原文稍有偏差。

如在理雅各译文中，译者分别用 Tsze-kung 翻译原文的"字"（子贡），Ts'ze 翻译原文的"名"（赐），体现了原文中"字"与"名"的差异，准确表达了原文所表达的人物关系。

1. **Tsze-kung** said, "What do you pronounce concerning the poor man who yet does not flatter, and the rich man who is not proud?" The Master replied, "They will do; but they are not equal to him, who, though poor, is yet cheerful, and to him, who, though rich, loves the rules of propriety."

2. **Tsze-kung** replied, "It is said in the *Book of Poetry*, 'As you cut and then file, as you carve and then polish.' —The meaning is the same, I apprehend, as that which you have just expressed."

The Master said, "With one like **Ts'ze**, I can begin to talk about the *Odes*. I told him one point, and he knew its proper sequence." （理雅各译）

---

① "《论语》1/15"指《论语》原文第一篇第十五章，以下同。

而在许渊冲的译文中，译者选择用同一个拼音 Zi Gong 翻译原文的"字"及"名"，未能充分体现原文所表达的《论语》编撰者与子贡之间及孔子与子贡之间的人物关系。

Zi Gong said, "What do you think of a poor man who does not flatter and a rich man who does not swagger?" The Master said, "Not bad, but not so good as a poor man who is cheerful and a rich man who is respectful." Zi Gong said, "Are such men like polished ivory and stone and jade refined, as said in the *Book of Poetry*?" The Master said, "My dear Zi Gong, now I may begin to talk with you about poetry. For when I told you about the past, you can anticipate the future." （许渊冲译）

（二）《论语》英译中的语内翻译及语际翻译

Jakobson（1971：261）将翻译分为三类：语内翻译（intralingual translation）、语际翻译（interlingual translation）、符际翻译（intersemiotic translation）。语内翻译指的是在同一种语言之内以同一语言的某种语言符号去翻译或解释另一种语言符号；语际翻译是指在两种语言之间用某一种语言符号去翻译或解释另一种语言符号；符际翻译是指用一些非语言符号去翻译或解释语言符号，或相反，用一些语言符号去翻译或解释非语言符号（转引自黄国文，2012：64）。

在《论语》英译中，历来都存在着对其中涉及的典故、事件、人物、语言等的不同理解和解释问题。当学界对典籍本身的解释存在争议时，译者通常根据自己的学识、翻译的目的、读者对象以及自己的价值取向和个人的翻译动机等因素，合理、合适、有选择地运用有关专家学者的研究成果，选取自己认为能够自圆其说的观点，并将之在译文翻译过程中体现出来。在《论语》从古文到英文的翻译过程中，包含了一个重要的不可忽略的过程，即《论语》从原文到现代汉语的语内翻译过程，包括对现有的语内翻译成果（包括对典籍中的一些事件、词句、段落的考究和解释、注解）的理解与取舍过程。

现有的《论语》语内翻译成果，即《论语》的今译版本，主要有以下四种：

1. 杨伯峻，《论语译注（简体字本）》，北京：中华书局，2006。
2. 李泽厚，《论语今读》，北京：生活·读书·新知三联书店，2004。
3. 钱穆，《论语新解》，北京：九州出版社，2011。
4. 天宜，《论语明心》，南京：东南大学出版社，2010。

不同的语内翻译版本，对于相同的《论语》原文语篇，有不同的翻译和诠释。比如，对于《论语》第九篇第一章原文"子罕言利与命与仁"（《论语》9/1），现有四种不同的语内翻译版本，如下所示：

1. 孔子很少（主动）谈到功利、命运和仁德。（杨伯峻，2006：98）

2. 孔子平日少言利，只赞同命与仁。（钱穆，2011：206）

3. 孔子很少讲利。许命，许仁。（李泽厚，2004：243）

4. 子罕在论及利的时候，总是能够和命和仁联系起来考虑。（天宜，2010：131）

而英译者所参照的不同语内翻译版本，将直接影响其语际翻译的不同，如下所示：

1. The subjects of which the Master seldom spoke were—profitableness, and also the appointments of Heaven, and perfect virtue.（理雅各译）

2. Confucius in his conversation seldom spoke of interests, of religion or of morality.（辜鸿铭译）

3. The Master seldom spoke of profit or fate or Goodness.（威利译）

4. Confucius rarely talked about lucre, but he had a great esteem for the will of God and virtue of humanity.（宋德利译）

5. Confucius seldom talked about gains, and yet he was for heavenly principles and benevolence.（王福林译）

6. Confucius seldom spoke of profit. He ascribed to destiny, he ascribed to benevolence.（张威麟译）

7. The Master seldom talked about what was profit or fate or benevolence.（许渊冲译）

对于"子罕言利与命与仁"这一"无定论"语内翻译的原文语篇，英译者如何通过阅读、吸收有关专家所做出的"语内翻译"（包括注释、评论等），并根据自己的学识、翻译的目的、翻译的动机等因素做出选择，再将汉语的文本转换成外（英）文，实现典籍翻译的语际翻译过程，是典籍英译工作的另一个难点。

三、翻译练习

（一）将下列英文书名和标题翻译为中文

1. *The Book of Poetry*

2. *The Confucian Analects*

3. *Strategies of the Warring States*

4. *The Works of Mencius*

5. *Historical Records*

6. *Book of Master Zhuang*

7. *Peach-Blossom Source*

8. *History of the Three Kingdoms*

（二）将下面的英文翻译为中文

1. Those who labour with their minds govern others; those who labour with their strenghs are governed by others.

2. Honest advice, though unpleasant to the ear, benefits conduct, just as bitter medicine cures sickness.

3. Opportunities of time vouchsafed by Heaven are not equal to advantages of situation afforded by the Earth, and advantages of situation afforded by the Earth are not equal to the union arising from the accord of Men.

4. To worry before all the people are worried and be delighted after the delight of all the people.

5. Think thrice before you act.

6. To be insatiable in learning and be tireless in teaching.

第二章 《论语》原文与现代英语的句式比较及其翻译

本章通过具体的实例，探讨《论语》原文与英文在句法结构上的相似之处及主要差异，以及《论语》英译中通常采取的翻译策略和技巧。

一、原文与英文句法结构的主要相似点及其翻译

（一）原文判断句 VS 英语 SVC 句型

《论语》原文为中文文言文，而中文文言文通常用"者"或"也"表判断，或用判断动词"为""是"表判断，或用副词"乃""则""即""皆""耳"或否定副词"非"等表判断（郭著章等，2008：24）。大部分《论语》原文中的判断句可直接译为英语中的 SVC（即主语 + 谓语 + 补语）句型。例如：

例 1.
[原文]
今之孝者，是谓能养。（《论语》2/7）
[英译]（1）The duty of a good son nowadays means only to be able to support his parents. （辜鸿铭译）

（2）The filial piety of nowadays means the support of one's parents. （理雅各译）

（3）Filial sons of today only take care their parents are well fed. （许渊冲译）

例 2.
[原文]
子曰："古之学者为己，今之学者为人。"（《论语》14/24）
[英译]
Confucius remarked："Men in old times educated themselves for their own sakes, men now educate themselves to impress others."（辜鸿铭译）

（二）《论语》原文被动句 VS 英语被动结构

在文言文中，被动句主要有两种句型：一种是以一些被动词为标志的被动句型，如"于""受……于""见""为……所"等字所引出的被动结构；另一种是无标志的被动句型，相当于省略了被动句的标志词（郭著章等，2008：25）。这两种被动结构均可直接译为英文的被动结构。例如：

例 3：
[原文]
子曰："三军可夺帅也，匹夫不可夺志也。"（《论语》9/26）
[英译]

（1）Confucius remarked："The general of an army may be carried off, but a man of the common people cannot be robbed of his free will. "（辜鸿铭译）

（2）The three armies, said the Master, may be deprived of their commander-in-chief, but the common people cannot be deprived of his opinion. （许渊冲译）

二、原文与英文句法结构的主要差异及其翻译

（一）形合与意合

汉语和英语两种语言在句法结构上存在较大差异，主要体现在：汉语重意合，多用有灵名词作主语，重视篇章的整体结构，讲究起承转合和完整性，注重对称平衡；英语重形合，多用无灵名词做主语，强调篇章句式结构的严谨（郭著章等，2008：28）。

意合（parataxis），指词与词、句子与句子之间的组合在外部形态上没有明显的标记，而主要依靠意义上的关联来"黏合"；表现为不用或少用连接词。通常采用语序、词语本身、词汇接应、结构平行、重叠形式、重复等"黏合"手段进行意合。形合（hypotaxis），指句子与词组在外部形态上有明显的标记，当形态标记不充分时，还可用其他语法手段来显示词组、句子、句群中各成分之间的相互关系，多用连词、分词、动名词、介词短语和不定式等形式来表示句子与句子之间的关系（郭著章等，2008：28）。在《论语》英译中，译者可根据具体上下文分别采用意合法或形合法。例如：

例 4.

[原文]

子曰："不患人之不己知，患其不能也。"（《论语》14／32）

[英译]

（1）Be not afraid, said the Master, that you are unknown, but that you are unable.（许渊冲译）

（2）Confucius remarked："Be not concerned that men do not know you; be concerned that you have no ability."（辜鸿铭译）

（3）The Master said, "I will not be concerned at men's not knowing me; I will be concerned at my own want of ability."（理雅各译）

在三个译文中，许渊冲通过连词"but"的使用，采用形合的英语句式翻译原文意合的句型；在辜鸿铭和理雅各的译文中，译者通过标点符号的恰当使用，采用意合法，翻译原文意合的句型。其实英语也具有某些意合的特征，只是不那么明显。英语中的意合主要通过标点符号、省略等形式来实现。译者可根据具体的翻译实际，采用相应的句式结构来翻译原文。

（二）动词优势与名词、介词、分词优势

汉语句子中的动词没有形态变化，使用方便，多个动词在句中有相同地位；而英语句子则主要采用主谓结构，谓语动词有词形变化，且一个句子只有一个谓语动词，其他动词要借助名词来表达，名词与名词之间要靠介词来联系，因此英语是名词、介词和分词占主导地位的语言。在《论语》英译过程中，译者要抓住句子的主要动词，其余动词要用名词、介词和分词来处理（郭著章等，2008：31）。例如：

例 5.

[原文]

子曰："默而识之，学而不厌，诲人不倦，何有于我哉！"（《论语》7／2）

[英译]

Confucius then went on to say, "To meditate in silence; patiently to acquire knowledge; and to be indefatigable in teaching it to others：which one of these things can I say that I have done?"（辜鸿铭译）

对原文包含的三个动词结构"默而识之""学而不厌""诲人不倦"，译者在译文中通过三个并列的动名词形式表现出来，符合英文句式的习惯和要求。又如：

11

例 6.

[原文]

子曰："德之不修，学之不讲，闻义不能徙，不善不能改，是吾忧也。"（《论语》7/3）

[英译]

Lastly, Confucius said, "Neglect of godliness; study without understanding; failure to act up to what I believe to be right; and inability to change bad habits: these are things which cause me constant solicitude." （辜鸿铭译）

原文中的"修""讲""徙""改"等动词，在译文中分别用名词或名词词组"neglect""understanding""failure to act up""inability to change"来体现。

（三）重复与替代

汉英两种语言在代词的使用上差异很大。汉语中代词用得少，重复使用名词比较常见。而英语则一般避免重复某个词语，当需要重复某个词语的时候，一般要用代词或其他手段来避免重复。在《论语》英译过程中，译者要在适当的地方增加代词，避免名词的重复，特别是要增添合适的人称代词、物主代词、反身代词和关系代词，才能符合英语语言的表达习惯（郭著章等，2008：32）。例如：

例 7.

[原文]

君子务本，本立而道生。（《论语》1/2）

[英译]

The superior man bends his attention to what is radical. That being established, all practical courses naturally grow up. （理雅各译）

原文重复用两个名词"本"。译文中，第二个"本"用代词"that"代替，避免重复。

例 8.

[原文]

子曰："由，诲女知之乎？知之为知之，不知为不知，是知也。"（《论语》2/17）

[英译]

The Master said, "Yû, shall I teach you what knowledge is? When you know a thing, to hold that you know it; and when you do not know a thing, to allow that you do not know it; —that is knowledge." （理雅各译）

原文不断重复"知"与"之"。在理雅各译文中，"知"被分别译为名词knowledge 和动词know，而"之"的译文，在第一次出现时译作名词"a thing"，第二次出现时即改为代词 it，遵循了英语的习惯。又如：

例9.

[原文]

子曰："后生可畏，焉知来者之不如今也？四十、五十而无闻焉，斯亦不足畏也已。"（《论语》9/22）

[英译]

Confucius remarked, "Youths should be respected. How do we know that their future will not be as good as we are now? Only when a man is forty or fifty without having done anything to distinguish himself, does he then cease to command respect. "（辜鸿铭译）

原文中，"来者"是指前文出现的"后生"，"今"指的是当今时代的人；在译文中，由于"来者"所指代的人在前文已经出现过，所以用代词"their"来指代，"今"用代词"we"来指代。原文"四十、五十而无闻"前省略的主语在译文中用名词"a man"来替代，再次出现时就用"himself""he"来替代。

例10.

[原文]

子曰："父母在，不远游，游必有方。"（《论语》4/19）

[英译]

Confucius remarked, "While his parents are living, a son should not go far abroad; if he does, he should let them know where he goes. "（辜鸿铭译）

原文表达子女在父母在世的时候不远行，若不得已要远行，也应该告知具体的方位和去处。原文"不远游"前省略了主语名词"子女"，在翻译成英文时，完整的英文句子必须有主语，因此英文中增添了相应的名词"a son"，并在第二次及第三次出现时，用代词"his"和"he"来代替。

（四）省略与完备

汉语文言表意模糊，强调篇章的整体结构，讲究起承转合，注重对称平衡；而英语则表意准确，强调篇章句式结构的严谨。因此，在汉译英时，要进行必要的增译，增补省略的词句，使之结构严谨、意思完备（郭著章等，2008：34）。例如：

例 11.

[原文]

子曰："见贤思齐焉，见不贤而内自省也。"（《论语》4/17）

[英译]

Confucius remarked, "When we meet with men of worth, we should think how we may equal them. When we meet with worthless men, we should turn into ourselves and find out if we do not resemble them. "

原文省略了主语及宾语，译文增添了代词"we"做主语，"them"做宾语。

例 12.

[原文]

子曰："三年学，不至于谷，不易得也。"（《论语》8/12）

[英译]

（1）It is not easy to find a man who has learned for three years without thinking of becoming an official.（理雅各译）

（2）Confucius remarked, "A man who educates himself for three years without improvement is seldom to be found. "（辜鸿铭译）

原文句子省略了"三年学"的主语，译文中补充了名词"a man"做主语，使译文通顺达意。

（五）正说反译/反说正译法

negation 作为一种翻译技巧，主要指在翻译实践中，为了使译文忠实而合乎语言习惯地传达原文的意思，有时必须把原文中的肯定说法变成译文中的否定说法，或把原文中的否定说法变成译文中的肯定说法。例如：

例 13.

[原文]

子曰："君子不重，则不威；学则不固。主忠信。无友不如己者。过则勿惮改。"（《论语》1/8）

[英译]

（1）An intelligentleman, said the Master, should not be frivolous, or he would lack solemnity in his behavior and solidity in his learning. He should be truthful and faithful, and befriend his equals. He should not be afraid of admitting and amending his faults.（许渊冲译）

（2）Comfucius rematked，"A wise man who is not serious will not imspire respect；what hw learns will not remain permanet.

"Make conscientiousness and sincerity your first princides.

"Have no friends who are not as yourself.

"When you have bad habits do not hecitate to change them."

（3）The Master said，'If the scholar be not grave, he will not call forth any veneration，and his learning will not be solid.

'Hold faithfulness and sincerity as first principles.

'Have no friends not equal to yourself.

'When you have fault，do not fear to abandon them.'

对于原文"无友不如己者"的翻译，许渊冲译文采取了"反说正译"的方法，译文采用肯定的表达形式："befriend his equals"。而辜鸿铭的译文"Have no friends who are not as yourself"及理雅各的译文"Have no friends not equal to yourself"则采用与原文相同的"反说"方式来表达，即"反说正译法"。

三、翻译练习

将下列句子翻译成英文

1. 子曰："三军可夺帅也，匹夫不可夺志也。"
2. 君子坦荡荡，小人常戚戚。
3. 工欲善其事，必先利其器。
4. 三人行必有我师焉，择其善者而从之，其不善者而改之。
5. 温故而知新，可以为师矣。
6. 君子不以言举人，不以人废言。
7. 己所不欲勿施于人。
8. 无友不如己者。
9. 后生可畏。
10. 父母在，不远游，游必有方。

第三章 《论语》中关于"学"的论述及其译文赏析

本章主要通过具体的实例，赏析不同译者对《论语》中关于"学"的论述的英文译文。孔子是大学问家，他在学问上所取得的成就及他的治学方法，值得后人借鉴和学习（杨玉英，2013：101）。通过鉴赏《论语》中关于治学的论述、中国学者对于《论语》内涵的语内翻译（以下简称"今译"）及其各译者的英文翻译，学习孔子和弟子们的学习态度以及具体的学习方法，探讨不同译者对孔子在原文中所表达的治学思想的不同解释与翻译。

一、翻译实例与赏析

例1.
［原文］
子曰："学而时习之，不亦说乎？"（《学而》1/1）
［今译］
孔子说："学了，然后按一定的时间去实习它，不也高兴吗？"（杨伯峻译）
［英译］
（1）Is it not pleasant to learn with a constant perseverance and application?（理雅各译）
（2）To learn and at due times to repeat what one has learnt, is that not after all a pleasure?（威利译）
（3）It is indeed a pleasure to acquire knowledge and, as you go on acquiring, to put into practice what you have acquired.（辜鸿铭译）
（4）Is it not a delight to acquire knowledge and put it into practice?（许渊冲译）
（5）"To learn," said the Master, "and then to practice opportunely what one has learnt—does not this bring with it a sense of satisfaction?"（詹宁斯译）

此为《论语》开篇的第一句话，点明了孔子的治学之道。如朱熹在《论语集注》中所述，此篇为"入道之门、积德之基、学者之先务"，但对于"学而时习之"这一句话的诠释，在中文学者中存有不同的争议，体现在英文译文中，更是各有不同。

由于《论语》原文的开放性特征，不同学者对原文有不同的诠释。根据杨伯峻的解释，"时"字在周秦时代做副词的时候，表示"在一定的时候"或"在适当的时候"的意思（杨伯峻，2006：2），因此，杨伯峻将"学而时习之，不亦说乎"今译为"学了，然后按一定的时间去实习它，不也高兴吗"；而朱熹将"学而时习之"解释为"习，鸟数飞也。学之不已，如鸟数飞也……既学而又时时习之，则所学者熟，而中心喜说"（朱熹，1992：1）。根据朱熹的解释，"时习之"的"时"，是"时时"的意思。参照不同的语内翻译版本，不同的英译本对原文的内涵也有不同的体现。

以上五种翻译的主要差异体现在对"时习之"的翻译上。理雅各将其译为 constant perseverance and application，威利将其译为 at due times to repeat，詹宁斯将其译为 practice opportunely，辜鸿铭和许渊冲在译文中省略原文"时"的意思，仅译出"习"，因而将其译为 put into practice。理雅各将"时"译为 constant，应该是受朱熹注释的影响，而威利将"时"译为 at due times，詹宁斯将其译为 opportunely，将原文诠释为"学习，然后在适当的时候去实习所学的知识"，比较符合人性和事物发展的规律，较为接近《论语》原文的意义内涵（姜哲，2013：49）。

例2.

[原文]

曾子曰："吾日三省吾身……传不习乎？"（《论语》1/4）

[今译]

（1）曾子说："我每天多次自己反省……老师传授我的学业是否复习了呢？"（杨伯峻译）

（2）曾子说："我每天多次反省自己……所传授给别人的东西，自己实践过吗？"（李泽厚译）

[英译]

（1）The philosopher Tsang said, "I daily examine myself on three points…whether I may have not mastered and practiced the instructions of my teacher. "（理雅各译）

（2）Master Tseng said, Every day I examine myself on these three points…Have I failed to repeat the precepts that have been handed down to me?（威利译）

（3）A disciple of Confucius remarked, "I daily examine into my personal conduct on three points…Thirdly, whether I have not failed to practice what I profess in my teaching. "（辜鸿铭译）

（4）I ask myself, said Master Zeng, three questions every day…In teaching students, have I not put into practice what I teach them?（许渊冲译）

不同学者对"传不习乎"有不同的理解；从以上不同的英译可看出，不同译者对原文也有不同的诠释。理雅各与威利的英译所体现的意思与杨伯峻的今译所诠释之意相近，而辜鸿铭及许渊冲的译文与李泽厚的今译所表达的意思相近。不同译者在典籍翻译中所经过的语内翻译过程，或者译者所参考的语内翻译版本不同，会导致不同语际翻译版本的产生。

例 3.
[原文]
子曰："君子食无求饱，居无求安，敏于事而慎于言，就有道而正焉，可谓好学也已。"（《论语》1/14）

[今译]

（1）孔子说："君子，吃食不要求饱足，居住不要求舒适，对工作勤劳敏捷，说话却谨慎，到有道的人那里去匡正自己，这样，可以说是好学了。"（杨伯峻译）

（2）夫子说："君子吃饭不求饱足，居住不求舒适，做事敏捷，说话谨慎，向有道行者学习，规正自己的言行；这样，就可以说是好学的了。"（天宜译）

[英译]

（1）The Master said, "He who aims to be a man of complete virtue, in his food does not seek to gratify his appetite, nor in his dwelling-place does he seek the appliances of ease; he is earnest in what he is doing, and careful in his speech; he frequents the company of men of principle that he may be rectified; —such a person may be said indeed to love to learn. "（理雅各译）

（2）Confucius remarked, " A wise and good man, in matters of food, should never seek to indulge his appetite; in lodging, he should not be too solicitous of comfort. He should be diligent in business and careful in speech. He should seek for the company of men of virtue and learning, in order to profit by their lessons and example. In this way he may become a man of real culture. "（辜鸿铭译）

（3）An intelligentleman, said the Master, eats to live, and not lives to eat. He may dwell in comfort, but not seek comfort in dwelling. He should be prompt in action and cautious in speech. He should seek good company and amend his faults. Such a man may be said to be good at learning. （许渊冲译）

这种对"好学"的阐释，与一般人勤奋学习以追求较好的物质生活享受有所不同。孔子认为"好学"即不求物质生活的享受，而重视精神品格的提升。

对此语篇，不同译者采取不同的翻译方法，产生了不同的译文。

原文"食无求饱，居无求安"及"敏于事而慎于言"采用对偶的修辞手法，使原文形式整齐对称，读起来朗朗上口。原文使用字数相等、句法相似的语句来表现主题，译文可采用相似的修辞方式达到类似的修辞效果，或者采用意译的方式仅将原文的意思表达出来。许渊冲采用回环的修辞手法，如"eats to live, and not lives to eat"和"dwell in comfort, but not seek comfort in dwelling"来表达原文对偶修辞手法所表达的语言均衡感和节奏感，整篇翻译尽量做到和原文一样对仗工整。理雅各和辜鸿铭摒弃了原文的对仗结构，采用意译的方法，将原文所表达的意思表述出来。

例 4.

［原文］

子曰："温故而知新，可以为师矣。"（《论语》2/11）

［今译］

（1）孔子说："在温习旧知识时，能有新体会、新发现，就可以做老师了。"（杨伯峻译）

（2）孔子说："温习过去，以知道未来，这样便可以做老师了。"（李泽厚译）

［英译］

（1）One who can learn something new while reviewing what he has learned, said the Master, is fit to be a teacher. （许渊冲译）

（2）The Master said, "If a man keeps cherishing his old knowledge, so as continually to be acquiring new, he may be a teacher of others. "（理雅各译）

（3）Confucius remarked, "If a man will constantly go over what he has acquired and keep continually adding to it new acquirements, he may become a teacher of men. "（辜鸿铭译）

在这一篇章中，孔子认为学习应该"温故而知新"，善于从老师讲的旧知识、本人或同代人做的旧事的温习中琢磨出新的认识和感悟，认识过去，举一反三，触类旁通，提升自己，启发旁人（天宜，2010：18）。

原文的"温故而知新"是"可以为师矣"的条件，"温故"与"知新"可以理解为并列关系，两个动作处于并列地位；也可以理解为主从关系，"知新"为"温故"之目的或结果，不同的今译版本已然体现了不同译者对此的不同诠释。在各版本英译文中，辜鸿铭译文用 and 表达了"温故"和"知新"的并列关系；理雅各译文中用 so as to 表述"知新"为"温故"的目的；许渊冲译文使用 while 连接 learn something 与 reviewing what he has learned，译文表述的重点放在动词"知新"上，强调一个人要是在"温故"的时候能够"知新"，这样就可以当老师了。许渊冲译文所表达的意思与杨伯峻的今译对原文的诠释相近，体现了许渊冲在翻译过程中参考了现代汉语的版本和已经出版的英译文，这点他在"首届《论语》翻译研讨会"的问答中也曾提及："《论语》英语翻译主要参考了四部我国或英国学者的

著作，分别是杨伯峻、李泽厚、理雅各和威利。"（吴国向，2012：106）

例 5.

[原文]

子曰："由！诲女知之乎！知之为知之，不知为不知，是知也。"（《论语》2/17）

[今译]

（1）夫子说："由，我教你求知的正确途径吧。知道的就是知道的，不知道的就是不知道的，这才是明智的。"（天宜译）

（2）孔子说："由！教给你对待知或不知的正确态度吧！知道就是知道，不知道就是不知道，这就是聪明智慧。"（杨伯峻译）

（3）孔子说："子路，我告诉你什么叫求知吧，知道就是知道，不知道就是不知道，这就是真正的'知道'"。（李泽厚译）

[英译]

（1）The Master said, "Yû, shall I teach you what knowledge is? When you know a thing, to hold that you know it; and when you do not know a thing, to allow that you do not know it; —this is knowledge. "（理雅各译）

（2）Confucius said to a disciple, "Shall I teach you what is understanding? To know what it is that you know, and to know what it is that you do not know, —that is understanding. "（辜鸿铭译）

（3）Shall I teach you what knowledge is? Said the Master to Zi Lu, to admit what you know and what you do not know, that is knowledge.（许渊冲译）

"由"，姓仲名由，字子路，是孔子早年的学生。朱熹说，仲由好勇，有强不知以为知的毛病，所以孔子这样教导他（天宜，2010：21）。对于原文"是知也"的解读，杨伯峻（2006：20）认为"知"同"智"，"是知也"应译为："这就是对待知或不知的正确态度。"

将原文"知之为知之，不知为不知，是知也"的三个英译文回译成中文，可看出不同译者对原文的理解有所差异。

理雅各的译文"When you know a thing, to hold that you know it; and when you do not know a thing, to allow that you do not know it; —this is knowledge"可回译为："知道就说你知道；不知道，也要允许你不知道——这才是真知识。"

许渊冲的译文"To admit what you know and what you do not know, that is knowledge"可回译为："承认你所知道的和不知道的，这才是真知识。"

辜鸿铭的译文"To know what it is that you know, and to know what it is that you do not know, —that is understanding"可回译为："理解你所知道的知识，也理解你现在还不知道的知识，这才是真正的理解。"

通过将英译文回译成中文，可看出理雅各和许渊冲译文表达的意思与杨伯峻和天宜对原文的理解相近；而辜鸿铭英译中表达的意思则与李泽厚的今译相近，表达"人贵有自知之明"之意，告诉人们，人只有在认识自己"不知"时，才有可能"知"。

例6.
[原文]
子曰："三人行，必有我师焉：择其善者而从之，其不善者而改之。"（《论语》7/22）
[英译]
（1）The Master said,"When I walk along with two others, they may serve me as my teachers. I will select their good qualities and follow them, their bad qualities and avoid them."（理雅各译）
（2）Confucius remarked,"When three men meet together, one of them who is anxious to learn can always learn something of the other two. He can profit by the good example of the one and avoid the bad example of the other."（辜鸿铭译）
（3）When three men walk together, said the Master, there must be one worthy to be my teacher. I will choose what is good in him to follow, and avoid what is not good.（许渊冲译）

"三人行，必有我师焉"，是家喻户晓、妇孺皆知、耳熟能详的孔子明训。孔子是天下最善于取人之长的好学者，而且明于借鉴、学人之善、改人之过（天宜，2010：106）。《论语集注》将原文"三人行"解释为"三人同行，其一我也。彼二人者，一善一恶，则我从其善而改其恶焉。是二人者，皆我师也"（朱熹，1992：68）。即善、恶两种人都是老师，体现了孔子随时随处向人学习、择善而从的思想。而有些学者认为，原文表达的意思是"即使只有两人同行，也仍然有可以学习的对象和事情"（李泽厚，2004：209），不必机械地将"三人行"中的另外两人理解为善、恶两人。在不同的英译文中，译者对原文的诠释也有所不同。

以上三位译者的译文，体现其对原文"三人行"的不同理解与诠释。理雅各的译文从"I"的叙述角度出发，"我"，即原文的孔子，为三人之中的一人，意为"我"向其他两人学习。辜鸿铭的译文中，译者为置身事外的叙述者，"三人行"中有一位热衷于学习的人，他总能够在其他两人身上找到他可以学习的东西。而许渊冲的译文中，则出现了四个人物，"我"即原文的"孔子"，是"三人行"之外的另一人。

例7.

[原文]

子曰："学如不及，犹恐失之。"(《论语》8/17)

[今译]

孔子说："做学问好像追逐什么似的，生怕赶不上，赶上了，还生怕丢掉了。"（杨伯峻译）

[英译]

（1）The Master said，"Learn as if you could not reach your object，and were always fearing also lest you should lose it."（理雅各译）

（2）Confucius remarked，"In education study always as if you have not yet reached your goal and though apprehensive of losing it."（辜鸿铭译）

（3）Be eager to acquire knowledge，said the Master，as if it were beyond reach，as if you were afraid to lose it even when it is acquired.（许渊冲译）

"学如逆水行舟，不进则退。"孔子在本章中告诫弟子们，学习应该有紧迫感。"学如不及"，是指害怕来不及学习的紧迫感；"犹恐失之"，是指一种虽学有所成，但又怕因为根基不稳而疏忽遗忘的不安感（杨玉英，2013：105）。一个人真正好学，就应该具有紧迫感和不安感，不断地学习，抓住当下，不待明日，温故而知新。

例8.

[原文]

子曰："我非生而知之者，好古，敏以求之者也。"(《论语》7/20)

[今译]

（1）夫子说："我不是生下来就知道一切的人，是爱好古代传统，勤奋追求而取得学问的。"（天宜译）

（2）孔子说：我不是生来就有知识的，我的知识是爱好古代文化，再勤奋学习得来的。（杨玉英译）

[英译]

（1）The Master said，"I am not one who was born in the possession of knowledge；I am one who is fond of antiquity，and earnest in seeking it there."（理雅各译）

（2）Confucius remarked，"I am not one born with understanding. I am only one who has given himself to the study of antiquity and is diligent in seeking for understanding in such studies."（辜鸿铭译）

（3）I was not born with innate knowledge，said the Master. Fond of history，I am eager in pursuit of the experience accumulated in it.（许渊冲译）

在此章中孔子强调自己不是"生而知之者"，自己的知识是后天努力学习的结果，强调要孜孜不倦地学习。

例9.

[原文]

孔子曰："生而知之者，上也。学而知之者，次也。困而学之，又其次也。困而不学，民斯为下矣。"（《论语》16/9）

[今译]

孔子说："生来就懂得道理的，是上等人；经过学习而懂得道理的，是次一等的人；遇到困难再去学习的，是又次一等的人；遇到困难还不学习的，这种就是下等的愚人了!"（天宜译）

[英译]

（1）Confucius said, "Those who are born with the possession of knowledge are the highest class of men. Those who learn, and so, readily, get possession of knowledge, are the next. Those who are dull and stupid, and yet compass the learning, are another class next to these. As to those who are dull and stupid and yet do not learn; —they are the lowest of the people. "（理雅各译）

（2）Master K'ung said, highest are those who are born wise. Next are those who become wise by learning. After them come those who have to toil painfully in order to acquire learning. Finally, to the lowest class of common people belong those who toil painfully without ever managing to learn.（威利译）

（3）Highest are those born wise, said Confucius, next come those who become wise by learning, still next those who strive to learn, and last come those people who will not strive at all.（许渊冲译）

在本章中，孔子着重强调的是"学"，"生而知之者"毕竟是少数，多数人是"学而知之""困而学之"。孔子训导自己的学生，要好学、善学，不做下等愚人。

例10.

[原文]

子曰："古之学者为己，今之学者为人。"（《论语》14/24）

[今译]

孔子说："古代学者的目的在修养自己的学问道德，现代学者的目的却在装饰自己，给别人看。"（杨伯峻译）

[英译]

（1）The Master said, "In ancient times, men learned with a view to their own improvement. Nowadays, men learn with a view to the approbation of others. "（理雅各译）

（2）The Master said, in old days men studied for the sake of self-improvement; nowadays men study in order to impress other people. （威利译）

（3）Confucius remarked, "Men in old times educated themselves for their own sakes, Men now educate themselves to impress others." （辜鸿铭译）

在这一章中，孔子描述了古今、真假两种学者为学的不同目的：真学者注重自身道德修养，假学者注重门面、注重包装自己（天宜，2010：242）。而在不同的英译中，译者对于"为己"和"为人"的翻译也有所不同。回译成中文，理雅各表述的意思是：在古代，人们学习是为了提升自己，而如今，人们学习是为了得到其他人的认可和赞扬。

威利和辜鸿铭的译文，回译为：古代人学习是为了提升自己，而现今人们学习是为了让别人记住自己。

三个译文虽然在词语选择及句子结构上有所差异，但是都表达了原文所表现的两种为学者的不同学习目的。

例11.

[原文]

子曰："学而不思则罔，思而不学则殆。"（《论语》2/15）

[今译]

（1）孔子说："学习而不思考，迷惘；思考而不学习，危险。"（李泽厚译）

（2）夫子说："只学习书本而不联系实际思考就会迷惑，光是空思空想而不抓紧读书学习则有使学问落空的危险。"（天宜译）

[英译]

（1）The Master said, "Learning without thought is labour lost; thought without learning is perilous." （理雅各译）

（2）Confucius remarked, "Study without thinking is labour lost. Thinking without study is perilous." （辜鸿铭译）

（3）To learn without thinking, said the Master, risks to be blind, while to think without learning risks to be impractical. （许渊冲译）

（4）The Master said, "Learning without thinking leads to puzzlement; thinking without learning is perilous." （吴国珍译）

例 12.

[原文]

子曰: "不愤①不启, 不悱②不发。举一隅③不以三隅反, 则不复也。"(《论语》7/8)

[今译]

(1) 孔子说: "教导学生, 不到他想求明白而不得的时候, 不去开导他; 不到他想说出来却说不出来的时候, 不去启发他。教给他东方, 他却不能由此推知西、南、北三方, 便不再教他了。"(杨伯峻译)

(2) 孔子说: "不到他努力想懂而懂不了, 我不去开导, 不到他努力想说而说不出, 我不去引发。告诉他一个角落如此, 他不能随之联系到另外三个角落, 我就不再多说了。"(杨玉英译)

[英译]

(1) The Master said, "I do not open up the truth to one who is not eager to get knowledge, nor help out any one who is not anxious to explain himself. When I have presented one corner of a subject to any one, and he cannot from it learn the other three, I do not repeat my lesson. "(理雅各译)

(2) Confucius then went on to say: "In my method of teaching, I always wait for my student to make an effort himself to find his way through a difficulty, before I show him the way myself. I also make him find his own illustrations before I give him one of my own. When I have pointed out the bearing of a subject in one direction and found that my student cannot himself see its bearings into other directions, I do not then repeat my lesson. "(辜鸿铭译)

(3) I will not instruct, said the Master, those who are not eager to learn, nor enlighten those who are not anxious to discover. If I show a man one corner of the table and he cannot infer the other three, I will not repeat the lesson. (许渊冲译)

这句话阐述了孔子的 "启发式" 教学思想, 注重学生主动学习和理解的过程, 力求做到举一反三、触类旁通。

原文中的 "一隅" 有隐喻意义, 英译要根据具体情况, 采用直译、意译、直译意译相结合等译法。理雅各和许渊冲采取直译法, 保留原文中 "一隅" 的隐喻意义, 译文中 corner 也有原文的隐喻意义, 指 one aspect; 而辜鸿铭则采取意译法。

辜译中, bearing 表示 relevant relation or interconnection。

---

① 愤: 心求通而未得。

② 悱: 口欲言而未能。

③ 隅: 念 yú, 角落。

例 13.

[原文]

子曰："默而识之，学而不厌，诲人不倦，何有于我哉?"(《论语》7/2)

[今译]

孔子说：把所见所闻默默地记在心里，努力学习而不厌弃，教导别人而不疲倦，这些事情我做到了哪些呢？（杨伯峻译）

[英译]

（1）The Master said, "The silent treasuring up of knowledge; learning without satiety; and instructing others without being wearied: — what one of these things belongs to me?"（理雅各译）

（2）Confucius then went on to say, "To meditate in silence; patiently to acquire knowledge; and to be indefatigable in teaching it to others: which one of these things can I say that I have done?"（辜鸿铭译）

（3）If I can learn by heart, said the Master, not tired of learning nor of teaching, what more shall I need?（许渊冲译）

例 14.

[原文]

子曰："有教无类。"(《论语》15/39)

[今译]

孔子说："人人我都教育，没有（贫富、地域等）区别。"（杨伯峻译）

[英译]

（1）In education, said the Master, there should be no distinction of classes.（许渊冲译）

（2）Confucius remarked, "Among really educated men, there is no caste or race-distinction."（辜鸿铭译）

（3）The Master said, "Let there be education for all irrespective of learners' background."（吴国珍译）

例 15.

[原文]

子曰："中人以上，可以语上也；中人以下，不可以语上也。"(《论语》6/21)

[今译]

孔子说："中等水平以上的人，可以告诉他高深学问；中等水平以下的人，不可以告诉他高深学问。"（杨伯峻译）

[英译]

（1）The Master said, "To those whose talents are above mediocrity, the highest subjects may be announced. To those who are below mediocrity, the highest subjects may not be announced. "（理雅各译）

（2）We may talk about what goes beyond the understanding of the average, said the Master, with those who are above mediocrity, not with those who are below.（许渊冲译）

（3）The Master said, "To those above the average, advanced knowledge can be preached; to those below the average, no advanced knowledge shall be taught. "（吴国珍译）

此章体现了孔子"因材施教"的教学理念。

二、翻译练习与思考

（一）将下列句子翻译成英文

1. 学而时习之，不亦说乎？
2. 温故而知新，可以为师矣。
3. 学而不思则罔，思而不学则殆。
4. 知之为知之，不知为不知，是知也。
5. 三人行，必有我师焉。
6. 择其善者而从之，其不善者而改之。
7. 子在川上，曰："逝者如斯夫! 不舍昼夜。"
8. 子曰："吾尝终日不食，终夜不寝，以思，无益，不如学也。"
9. 子夏曰："日知其所亡，月无忘其所能，可谓好学也已矣。"
10. 子曰："默而识之，学而不厌，诲人不倦，何有于我哉?"

（二）思考与讨论

孔子关于"学"的论述，哪一个对你最有启发? 选出其中一个论述，查阅不同译者的译文并进行分析。你最喜欢哪一个? 为什么?

第四章　《论语》中关于"仁"的论述及其译文赏析

　　"仁"是孔子的核心思想，是孔子哲学中最高的德行标准，是各种美德融会贯通的最高境界。后代的学者往往以"仁"为孔子的一贯之道，甚至称儒学为"仁学"。整部《论语》共有59章提到"仁"，一共出现了109个"仁"字，但是《论语》中没有一章给"仁"下过明确的定义。弟子们向孔子请教"仁"的问题时，孔子因材施教，给每个人的回答都不一样，因为每个人的才华气质不同，进德修业的方向也不一样，所以孔子会很具体地针对不同的人和情况来启示人们如何实现"仁"。

　　本章通过赏析《论语》原文及译文中关于"仁"的论述，探讨《论语》中"仁"的思想及其在英译文中的体现。

一、翻译实例与赏析

　　例1.
　　［原文］
　　孝弟①也者，其为仁之本与！（《论语》1/2）
　　［今译］
　　孝悌之道，它是仁道的根本啊！（天宜译）
　　［英译］
　　（1）Filial piety and fraternal submission! —are they not the root of all benevolent actions?（理雅各译）
　　（2）To be a good son and a good citizen—do not these form the foundation of a moral life?（辜鸿铭译）
　　（3）Respect for one's parents and elder brothers is the fundamental quality for a good man.（许渊冲译）
　　（4）Filial piety and fraternal love are the foundation of benevolence.（吴国珍译）

　　本章通过孔子的弟子有子之口，提出"孝弟也者，其为仁之本与"，即提出仁

---

　　① 弟（tì）：通"悌"，顺从和敬爱兄长。

学之本为孝悌之道。在《论语》中被称为"子"的孔门弟子，只有三人：有若、曾参和冉有。有若是孔子晚年的弟子，学得孔门真传。此仁学之根本由孔子的弟子说出来，说明孔子的仁学后继有人。

由于本章主要探讨"仁"的论述及其英译，以下笔者主要探讨译者对于"孝弟也者，其为仁之本与"的不同英译。

在几位译者的译文中，理雅各、许渊冲、吴国珍译文分别把"孝弟"翻译为filial piety and fraternal submission、respect for one's parents and elder brothers 以及 filial piety and fraternal love。其中，对"弟"的翻译，理雅各译文体现的是"对兄长的服从与尊敬"，而许渊冲译文所体现的是"对兄长的尊重"，吴国珍译文体现的是"对兄长的敬爱之情"，其所体现的含义稍有不同；许渊冲和吴国珍的译文，可能更符合现代读者对于"弟"字内涵的理解。

"仁"在几位译者的译文中，分别被译为 benevolent actions、a moral life、a good man 及 benevolence。理雅各将"仁"理解为一种善良的举动，因而在译文中选用 benevolent action 来翻译原文的"仁"，吴国珍的译文与之相近；而辜鸿铭则将其看作一种完美的道德品质，因而选用 a moral life 来翻译。许渊冲在其译文中，用 good 这个常用而具普遍意义的词来翻译在原文中反复出现的"仁"，将原文中"仁"的意义在译文中以较通俗化的方式展现出来。

例2.

[原文]

子曰："巧言令色，鲜矣仁！"（《论语》1/3）

[今译]

孔子说："花言巧语，伪善的面貌，这种人，'仁德'是不会多的。"（杨伯峻译）

[英译]

（1）The Master said, "Fine words and an insinuating appearance are seldom associated with true virtue."（理雅各译）

（2）Confucius remarked, "With plausible speech and fine manners will seldom be found moral character."（辜鸿铭译）

（3）A good man, said the Master, would rarely say what he does not believe, or pretend to appear better than he is.（许渊冲译）

上一章从积极的方面规定"仁之根本"，这一章从消极、否定的方面规定"仁"，强调"仁"不是指某种外在的华丽，指出外在的容色和语言都应该服从内在心灵的塑造（李泽厚，2004：29）。

在理雅各译文中，insinuating 的意思是 calculated to please or gain favor；insinuating appearance 比辜鸿铭的 fine manners 更能确切地表达原文"令色"的含义。

而辜鸿铭译文中的 plausible（意思是 seems likely to be true or valid）speech 比理雅各译文中的 fine words 更能表达原文中的"巧言"之意。许渊冲的译文，采取其一贯的典籍英译通俗化的翻译策略，采用常用的词语较好地诠释了"巧言令色"之意。

例3.

[原文]

子曰："里仁①为美。择不处②仁，焉得知？"（《论语》4/1）

[今译]

（1）孔子说："住的地方，要有仁德这才好。选择住处，没有仁德，怎么能是聪明呢？"（杨伯峻译）

（2）夫子说："与仁者为邻最好。选择住处而不选在仁者居住之处，怎能说是明智呢？"（天宜译）

[英译]

（1）The Master said, "It is virtuous manners which constitute the excellence of a neighbourhood. If a man in selecting a residence, do not fix on one where such prevail, how can he be wise?"（理雅各译）

（2）Confucius remarked, "It is the moral life of a neighbourhood which constitutes its excellence. He is not an intelligent man, who, in choosing his residence, does not select a place with a moral surrounding. "（辜鸿铭译）

（3）Good neighborhood, said the Master, adds beauty to life. If a man does not choose good neighborhood, how can he be called wise?（许渊冲译）

[讨论]

对于原文"里仁为美"的翻译，哪位译者的翻译最确切？许渊冲的译文是否与原文的意义有不对等的地方？体现了作者哪种翻译理念？这些问题值得思考。

例4.

[原文]

子曰："不仁者，不可以久处约，不可以长处乐。仁者安仁，知者利仁。"（《论语》4/2）

---

① 里仁：指居住在仁者所居住的地方；"里"做动词。

② 处：居住。

[今译]

（1）孔子说："不仁的人不可以长久地居于穷困中，也不可以长久地居于安乐中。有仁德的人安于仁（实行仁德便心安，不实行仁德心便不安），聪明人利用仁（他认识到仁德对他长远而巨大的利益，他便实行仁德）。"（杨伯峻译）

（2）孔子说："不仁的人不能够长久地处在贫困之中，不能够长期地处在安乐之中。仁德的人行仁安仁，明智的人用仁行仁。"（天宜译）

[英译]

（1）The Master said, "Those who are without virtue, cannot abide long either in a condition of poverty and hardship, or in a condition of enjoyment. The virtuous rest in virtue; the wise desire virtue. "（理雅各译）

（2）Confucius remarked, "A man without moral character cannot long put up with adversity, nor can he long enjoy prosperity. "

"Men of moral character find themselves at home in being moral; men of intelligence find it advantageous to be moral. "（辜鸿铭译）

（3）A man without virtue, said the Master, cannot endure adversity nor enjoy prosperity for long. A good man is content to be good; a wise man knows it pays to be good.（许渊冲译）

三种译文的区别主要体现在对原文"利仁"的不同理解及翻译上。根据《论语集注》："约，穷困也。利，犹贪也。盖深知笃好而必欲得之也。不仁之人，失其本心，久约必滥。惟仁者则安其仁而无适不然，知者则于仁而不易所守。盖虽深浅之不同，然皆非外物所能夺矣。"（朱熹1992：30）天宜（2010：45）认为，"利仁"指的是"利用仁行利民利国之举"；李泽厚（2004：107）认为，"利仁者，其见行仁者若于彼我皆利，则己行之"。理雅各将"知者利仁"译为the wise desire virtue，回译成中文为：智者渴望行仁。辜鸿铭的译文回译成中文，即为：智者发现行仁是有利的。许渊冲的译文回译为：智者知道行仁是值得的。通过译文的回译，我们可以看出，辜鸿铭和许渊冲的译文所表达的意思和原文更相近。

例5.

[原文]

子曰："唯仁者，能好①人，能恶②人。"（《论语》4/3）

[今译]

（1）孔子说："只有仁人才能够喜爱某人，厌恶某人。"（杨伯峻译）

---

① 好（hào）：喜爱。
② 恶（wù）：厌恶。

（2）先生说："只有仁者，能真心地喜好人，也能真心地厌恶人。"（钱穆译）

[英译]

（1）The Master said, "It is only the truly virtuous man, who can love, or who can hate, others. "（理雅各译）

（2）Confucius remarked, "It is only men of moral character who know how to love men or to hate men. "（辜鸿铭译）

（3）Only a benevolent man, said the Master, can love the good and dislike the wrong.（许渊冲译）

从常理看来，"好人恶人"，人孰不能？为何孔子特别强调"唯仁者，能好人，能恶人"呢？钱穆（2011：78）认为，此章语浅言深。不仁之人，心多私欲，因多谋求顾虑，遂使心之所好，不能真好，心之所恶，不能真恶。唯仁者其心明通，乃始能好人恶人。原文"好人"及"恶人"中的"人"没有具体化，是一个抽象的概念，体现了《论语》的"微言大义"。理雅各和辜鸿铭分别用同样的抽象代词others 和名词 men 来翻译"人"，而许渊冲则用具体的 the good 和 the wrong 把两个小句中"人"的含义具体化。三个译文回译成中文，理雅各的译文为：只有真正有德行的人，才能爱人，才能恨人。在英文的语境下，英文读者对译文所表达的意思可能也会心存"为何只有仁者才能爱人恨人"的疑虑。辜鸿铭的译文回译为：只有真正有德行的人才懂得如何爱人，如何恨人。辜鸿铭的译文更具体，使原文的意思更清晰地展示在读者面前。同样，许渊冲的译文也将原文的微言大义具体化，许渊冲的译文回译为：只有仁者，才能喜爱好人，憎恶坏人。

例6.

[原文]

（樊迟）问仁。曰："仁者先难而后获，可谓仁矣。"（《论语》6/22）

[今译]

（1）（樊迟）问如何是仁。孔子说："困苦艰难在先而酬报、果实在后，这就可以叫仁了。"（李泽厚译）

（2）（樊迟）问怎样做才可以达到仁。夫子说："仁人是难事做在人前，收获退居人后，可以说是有仁了。"（天宜译）

[英译]

（1）Fan Ch'ih asked about perfect virtue. The Master said, "The man of virtue makes the difficulty to be overcome his first business, and success only a subsequent consideration; —this may be called perfect virtue. "（理雅各译）

（2）The disciple then asked what constituted a moral life. Confucius answered, "A man who wants to live a moral life must first be conscious within himself of a difficulty and has struggled to overcome the difficulty: that is the definition or test of a moral life. "（辜鸿铭译）

（3）When Fan Chi asked about a good man, the Master said, "A good man will do hard work before he reaps. So may he be called a good man. "（许渊冲译）

本章中孔子告诫樊迟，"仁"就是以所难为先而不计所获，先为他人，后虑自己。

从三位译者的译文中可以看出，三位译者对原文的诠释各有不同。理雅各在译文里体现的意思是"一位仁者，通常首先考虑他需要克服的困难，而成功是他在此之后才加以考虑的范畴"。辜鸿铭的译文与理雅各的译文所体现的含义有所差异，辜鸿铭的译文所体现的意思是"一个人，如果要过一种有道德的生活，首先必须意识到他要克服的困难，而且付诸行动去克服此困难"。而许渊冲译文对于"先难而后获"的翻译回译成中文则是"先努力工作，然后再收获成果"。

例7.

[原文]

子贡问为仁。子曰："工欲善其事，必先利其器。居是邦也，事其大夫之贤者，友其士之仁者。"（《论语》15/10）

[今译]

（1）子贡问如何去实行"仁"。孔子说："工匠要干好他的制作，必先磨锐他的工具。住在一个国家里，就要事奉有贤德的官长，结交那些有仁德的知识分子。"（李泽厚译）

（2）子贡问怎样做到仁。夫子说："工匠要做好他的工作，一定要准备好精良的工具。居住在这个国家，要侍奉他们大夫中的贤者，结交他们士人中的仁者。"（天宜译）

[英译]

（1）Tsze-Kung asked about the practice of virtue. The Master said, "The mechanic, who wished to do his work well, must first sharpen his tools. When you are living in any State, take service with the most worthy among its great officers, and make friends of the most virtuous among its scholars. "（理雅各译）

（2）A disciple of Confucius enquired how to live a moral life. Confucius answered: "A workman who wants to perfect his work first sharpens his tools. When you are living in a country, you should serve those nobles and ministers in that country who are men of moral worth, and you should cultivate the friendship of the gentlemen of that country who are men of moral worth. "（辜鸿铭译）

（3）Zi Gong asked how to render good service. The Master said, "A craftsman who wishes to do his work well must first sharpen his tools. You who serve in a state must act in agreement with its good officers and befriend its good intellectuals. "（许渊冲译）

[讨论]

三位译者对"工欲善其事，必先利其器"的不同翻译，所体现的意义有何差异？

例8.

[原文]

（1）子曰："知者乐水，仁者乐山。知者动，仁者静。知者乐，仁者寿。"（《论语》6/23）

（2）子曰："知者乐，水；仁者乐，山。知者动，仁者静。知者乐，仁者寿。"（天宜：87）

[今译]

（1）先生说："知者喜好水，仁者喜好山。知者常动，仁者常静。知者常乐，仁者常寿。"（钱穆译）

（2）夫子说："智者的快乐，如水，仁者的快乐，如山。智者动中求静，仁者静中观动。智者快乐，仁者长寿。"（天宜译）

[英译]

（1）The Master said, "The wise find pleasure in water; the virtuous find pleasure in hills. The wise are active; the virtuous are tranquil. The wise are joyful, the virtuous are long-lived. "（理雅各译）

（2）Confucius remarked, "Men of intellectual character delight in water scenery; men of moral character delight in mountain scenery. Intellectual men are active; moral men are calm. Intellectual men enjoy life; moral men live long. "（辜鸿铭译）

（3）The wise, said the Master, delight in water while the good delight in mountains. The wise love mobility while the good love tranquility. The wise live happy while the good live long. （许渊冲译）

钱穆认为，在《论语》此章论述中，孔子指出：智者和仁者热爱大自然，享受快乐平和的生活。

对于原文的理解和标点方式，有学者（天宜，2010）提出了不同的诠释。

从三位译者的译文可看出，三位译者对于原文的诠释与钱穆的今译接近，而与天宜的诠释不同。注意三位译者对于原文"知者"与"仁者"的不同译文。

例 9.

[原文]

樊迟问仁。子曰:"爱人。"问知。子曰:"知人。"(《论语》12/22)

[今译]

樊迟问如何是"仁",孔子说:"爱人。"樊迟问如何是"知",孔子说:"了解别人。"(李泽厚译)

[英译]

(1) Fan Chi'h asked about benevolence. The Master said,"It is to love all men."He asked about knowledge. The Master said,"It is to know all man."(理雅各译)

(2) The same disciple mentioned above asked:"What does a moral life consist in?""The moral life of a man,"answered Confucius,"consists in loving men."

The disciple then asked,"What does understanding consist in?""Understanding,"answered Confucius,"consists in understanding men."(辜鸿铭译)

(3) Fan Chi asked about a good ruler. The Master said,"A good ruler loves the ruled."Fan Chi asked about a wise ruler. The Master said,"A wise ruler knows the ruled."(许渊冲译)

原文的抽象概念"爱人"在理雅各与辜鸿铭的译文中,分别体现为 love all men 及 loving men。而在许渊冲的译文中,"爱人"体现为 loves the ruled,"人"的概念由原文的泛指在译文中被具体化为"被统治阶层"。在许渊冲译的文中,"仁"被译为 a good ruler,指的是"做一个好的统治者",或"实行仁政的统治者",这与理雅各及辜鸿铭的诠释均有不同。

例 10.

[原文]

子曰:"刚、毅、木、讷,近仁。"(《论语》13/27)

[今译]

孔子说:"刚强,坚韧,朴实,寡言,接近于仁了。"(李泽厚译)

[英译]

(1) The Master said:"The firm, the enduring, the simple, and the modest are near to virtue."(理雅各译)

(2) Confucius remarked:"A man of strong, resolute, simple character approaches nearly to the true moral character."(辜鸿铭译)

(3) Strong and steady, said the Master, wooden and wordless, such a man is nearly a good man.(许渊冲译)

许渊冲译文注重译文的音韵美，采用头韵（alliteration）的修辞手法。

例11.

[原文]

子曰："当仁，不让于师。"（《论语》15/36）

[今译]

（1）孔子说："如果追求'仁'，对老师也不必谦让。"（李泽厚译）

（2）夫子说："面对推行仁德之事，就是对于老师也不谦让。"（天宜译）

[英译]

（1）The Master said："Let every man consider virtue as what devolves on himself. He may not yield the performance of it even to his teacher."（理雅各译）

（2）Confucius remarked："When the question is one of morality, a man need not defer to his teacher."（辜鸿铭译）

（3）A good man, said the Master, should not withdraw from being a better man than his teacher.（许渊冲译）

（4）The Master said, "Never wait for your teacher to go ahead of you when facing a just cause."（吴国珍译）

根据孔子的教义，弟子通常应该在老师面前表现得谦卑与尊重，但在此篇，孔子教育弟子，当面对合乎仁德的事时，就要坚决去做，就是在老师面前，也不必谦让。现代汉语里的"当仁不让"已成为四字成语，与《论语》里的原意稍微有所差别，意为"遇到应该做的事情，积极主动地担当起来，毫不推辞"。

例12.

[原文]

子曰："志士仁人，无求生以害仁，有杀身以成仁"。（《论语》15/9）

[今译]

孔子说："志士仁人不苟全性命而损害仁，宁肯牺牲生命来完成仁。"（李泽厚译）

[英译]

（1）The Master said, "The determined scholar and the man of virtue will not seek to live at the expense of injuring their virtue. They will even sacrifice their lives to preserve their virtue complete."（理雅各译）

（2）Confucius remarked："A gentleman of spirit or a man of moral character will never try to save his life at the expense of his moral character：he prefers to sacrifice his life in order to save his moral character."（辜鸿铭译）

（3）A wise good man, said the Master, will do no wrong to preserve his own life but sacrifice his life to do what is right. （许渊冲译）

三位译者对于原文中的"志士仁人""害仁""成仁"，在译文中选择了不同的词语来表示。

理雅各的译文中将"志士仁人"译为 the determined scholar and the man of virtue，辜鸿铭的译文将其译为 a gentleman of spirit or a man of moral character，许渊冲则将其译为 a wise good man。

对于原文中的"害仁""成仁"，理雅各将其译为 injuring their virtue 和 preserve their virtue complete；辜鸿铭将其译为 at the expense of his moral character 和 save his moral character；而许渊冲则将其译为 do no wrong 和 do what is right。

同时，在三种译文中，译者采用的句子结构也有所不同。理雅各与辜鸿铭基本保持了原文的结构形式，而许渊冲的译文将原文的两个句子译为一个句子，句子结构有所改变。

例 13.
［原文］
子曰："苟志于仁矣，无恶也。"（《论语》4/4）
［今译］
孔子说："真决心努力于仁，也就不会做坏事了。"（李泽厚译）
［英译］
（1）The Master said, "If the will be set on virtue, there will be no practice of wickedness. "（理雅各译）

（2）Confucius remarked, "If you fix your mind upon a moral life, you will be free from evil. "（辜鸿铭译）

（3）If a man, said the Master, has made up his mind to be good, he will do no wrong. （许渊冲译）

［讨论］
有人把本篇中的"恶"读作 wù，孔子的这句话被理解为"一旦真下决心做好人，就不会讨厌什么了"。如果这样理解的话，又该怎样翻译呢？

例 14.
［原文］
子曰："仁远乎哉？我欲仁，斯仁至矣。"（《论语》7/30）

[今译]

孔子说："仁很遥远吗？哪个人如真想要它，它就会来的。"（李泽厚译）

[英译]

（1）The Master said, "Is virtue a thing remote? I wish to be virtuous, and lo! virtue is at hand. "（理雅格译）

（2）Confucius then went on to remark, "Is moral life something remote or difficult? If a man will only wish to live a moral life — there and then his life becomes moral. "（辜鸿铭译）

（3）Are we far from benevolence? Said the Master. If we wish to be benevolent, then benevolence is within our reach. （许渊冲译）

朱熹《论语集注》指出："仁者，心之德，非在外也。放而不求，故有以为远者；反而求之，则即此而在矣，夫岂远哉？"

此篇中，孔子教导弟子们，一个人只要在日常生活中经常行仁，就能实现仁，行仁的过程比实现仁的终极目标更重要（吴国珍，2012：223）。

原文中"仁"出现了三次，同样的"仁"，在原文中表达不同的意义，可以表述一个概念，也可以表述一个动作。译文中对"仁"有不同的表述，这也体现出译者对原文的不同诠释。

例15.

[原文]

颜渊问仁。子曰："克己复礼为仁。一日克己复礼，天下归仁焉，为仁由己，而由人乎哉？"

颜渊曰："请问其目。"子曰："非礼勿视，非礼勿听，非礼勿言，非礼勿动。"颜渊曰："回虽不敏，请事斯语矣。"（《论语》12/1）

[今译]

颜回问如何是仁。孔子说："约束自己以符合礼制就是仁。有一天都这样做，那中国就都回到'仁'了。这样做全靠自己，还能凭靠别人吗？"颜回说："请问具体的途径。"孔子说："不符合礼制的事不看，不符合礼制的事不听，不符合礼制的事不说，不符合礼制的事不做。"颜回说："我虽然不勤勉，但一定依据这些话去做。"（李泽厚译）

[英译]

（1）Yen Yüan asked about perfect virtue. The Master said, "To subdue one's self and return to propriety, is perfect virtue. If a man can for one day subdue himself and return to propriety, all under heaven will ascribe perfect virtue to him. Is the practice of perfect virtue from a man himself, or is it from others?" Yen Yüan said, "I beg to ask the steps of that process." The Master replied, "Look not at what is contrary to propriety; listen not to what is contrary to propriety; speak not what is contrary to propriety; make no movement which is contrary to propriety."

Yen Yüan then said, "Though I am deficient in intelligence and vigour, I will make it my business to practise this lesson." (理雅各译)

(2) A disciple of Confucius, the favorite Yen Hui, inquired what constituted a moral life. Confucius answered, "Renounce yourself and conform to the ideal of decency and good sense."

"If one could only," Confucius went on to say, "live a moral life, renouncing himself and conforming to the ideal of decency and good sense for one single day, the world would become moral. To be moral, a man depends entirely upon himself and not upon others."

The disciple then asked for practical rules to be observed in living a moral life. Confucius answered:"Whatever things are contrary to the ideal of decency and good sense, do not look upon them. Whatever things are contrary to the ideal of decency and good sense, do not listen to them. Whatever things are contrary to the ideal of decency and good sense, do not utter them with your mouth. Lastly, let nothing in whatever things you do, act or move, be contrary to the ideal of decency and good sense." (辜鸿铭译)

(3) Yan Yuan asked about benevolence. The Master said, "A benevolent man will control himself in conformity with the rules of propriety. Once every man can control himself in conformity with the rules of propriety, the world will be in good order. Benevolence depends on oneself, not on others." Yan Yuan asked about the details. The Master said, "Do not look at anything nor listen to anything nor speak of anything nor do anything against the rules of propriety." Then Yan Yuan said, "Dull as I am, I would put your instruction into practice." (许渊冲译)

此篇为《论语》中最重要的篇章之一。有学者认为（李泽厚，2003：317），此篇说明了孔子将实践外在礼制化作内心欲求，融理欲于一体而成为情（人性，即仁）的具体过程。"仁"不是自然人欲，也不是克制或消灭这"人欲"的"天理"，而是约束自己（克己），使一切视听言动都符合礼制（复礼），从而产生人性情感（仁）。

[讨论]
原文"非礼勿视，非礼勿听，非礼勿言，非礼勿动"的含义及其不同英译。

例16.
[原文]
曾子曰："士，不可以不弘毅，任重而道远。仁以为己任，不亦重乎，死而后

已，不亦远乎。"（《论语》8/7）

[今译]

（1）曾子说："知识分子不可以不弘大而刚毅，因为责任重大，路途遥远，将仁作为自己的责任，这不是责任重大吗？到死才能终止，这不是路途遥远吗？"（李泽厚译）

（2）曾子说："读书人不可以不抱负远大，意志坚强，因为他担当的责任重大，行道的里程遥远。以实现仁作为自己肩负的责任，岂不是使命重大吗？为此要终生奋斗，岂不是历程遥远吗？"（天宜译）

[英译]

（1）The philosopher Tsăng said, "The scholar may not be without breadth of mind and vigorous endurance. His burden is heavy and his course is long. Perfect virtue is the burden which he considers it is his to sustain；—is it not heavy？Only with death does his course stop；—is it not long？"（理雅各译）

（2）A disciple of Confucius remarked, "An educated gentleman may not be without strength and resoluteness of character. His responsibility in life is a heavy one, and the way is long. He is responsible to himself for living a moral life; is that not a heavy responsibility？He must continue in it until he dies; is the way then not a long one？"（辜鸿铭译）

（3）Master Zeng said, "An intellectual should be strong and steady, for his duty is heavy and his journey will be long. Is it not a heavy duty to be a man of men？Is his journey not long which will not end until his death？"（许渊冲译）

[讨论]

请分析"士，不可以不弘毅"的不同译法，包括反说反译法与反说正译法。

"任重而道远"在现代汉语里已成为成语。在现代汉语里，该如何翻译此成语？

例17.

[原文]

子贡曰："如有博施于民而能济众，何如？可谓仁乎？"子曰："何事于仁！必也圣乎！尧、舜其犹病诸！夫仁者，己欲立而立人，己欲达而达人。能近取譬，可谓仁之方也已。"（《论语》6/30）

[今译]

子贡说："如果广泛地给人民以好处，从而能够普遍救济群众，怎么样？可以说是仁吗？"孔子说："这哪里是仁，应该是圣了。连尧舜都难做到。所谓仁，是说自己想站起来，就帮助别人站起来，自己想开拓发展，就帮助别人开拓发展。从近处做起，可以说是实行仁的方法。"（李泽厚译）

[英译]

（1）Tsze-kung said, "Suppose the case of a man extensively conferring benefits on the people, and able to assist all, what would you say of him? Might he be called perfectly virtuous?" The Master said , "Why speak only of virtue in connection with him! Must he not have the qualities of a sage? Even Yâo and Shun were still solicitous about this. "

"Now the man of perfect virtue, wishing to be established himself, seeks also to establish others; wishing to be enlarged himself, he seeks also to enlarge others. "

"To be able to judge of others by what is nigh in ourselves; —this may be called the art of virtue. "（理雅各译）

（2）A disciple once said to Confucius, "If there is a man who carries out extensively good works for the welfare of the people and is really able to benefit the multitude, what would you say of such a man: could he be called a moral character?"

"Why call him only a moral character," answered Confucius, "if one must call such a man by a name, one would call him a holy or sainted man. For, judged by the works of which you speak, even the ancient Emperors Yao and Shun felt their shortcomings. "

Confucius remarked, "A moral man in forming his character forms the character of others; in enlightening himself he enlightens others. It is a good method in attaining a moral life, if one is able to consider how one would see things and act if placed in the position of others. "（辜鸿铭译）

（3）Zi Gong asked whether it could be called virtue to do good to people and benefit them. The Master said, " It is more than virtue; it is the accomplishment of a sage. Even the earliest emperor could not boast of such accomplishment. What is virtue? To establish others as you would establish yourself, and help others to develop as you would help yourself to. To judge of others by what is in yourself, that is the way towards virtue. "（许渊冲译）

正如朱熹（1992：60）所说，"以己及人，仁者之心也"。

二、翻译练习与思考

（一）翻译练习：将下列句子和词组翻译为英文

1. 任重而道远。

2. 当仁，不让于师。

3. 巧言令色。

4. 里仁为美。

5. 工欲善其事，必先利其器。

6. 非礼勿视，非礼勿听，非礼勿言，非礼勿动。

7. 知者乐水，仁者乐山。

8. 知者动，仁者静。

9. 知者乐，仁者寿。

10. 仁者先难而后获。

（二）思考与讨论

练习（一）中的句子与词组来自《论语》，在现代依然经常被引用。这些句子和词组在现代汉语里的用法与《论语》原文中的用法是否有差异？该如何将其翻译成英文？

第五章 《论语》中关于"孝"的论述及其译文赏析

古人说"百善孝为先",圣人以孝治天下,孝是一个人立身处世最基本的品德。孔子和弟子们谈孝,认为孝道是实行一切道德的根本,所有的教化都从"孝"中产生出来。孔子认为,对父母要孝顺、孝敬、孝养。顺,就是事事都顺着父母,"无违";敬和养,更重要的是敬,只养不敬,与与人饲减养牲口无异。

本章通过赏析《论语》原文及译文中关于"孝"的论述,探讨《论语》中"孝"的思想及其在英译文中的体现。

一、翻译实例与赏析

例1.

[原文]

有子曰:"其为人也孝弟,而好犯上者,鲜矣;不好犯上,而好作乱者,未之有也。君子务本,本立而道生。孝弟也者,其为仁之本与!"(《论语》1/2)

[今译]

有子说:"做人孝敬父母,尊爱兄长,而喜欢冒犯上级官长的,少有。不喜欢冒犯上级而喜欢造反作乱的,从来没有。君子在根本上下功夫,根本建立好了,人道也就生发出来。孝敬父母、尊敬兄长,就是人的根本吧?"(李泽厚译)

[英译]

(1) The philosopher Yû said, "They are few who, being filial and fraternal, are fond of offending against their superiors. There have been none, who, not liking to offend against their superiors, have been fond of stirring up confusion.

"The superior man bends his attention to what is radical. That being established, all practical courses naturally grow up. Filial piety and fraternal submission! —are they not the root of all benevolent actions?"(理雅各译)

(2) A disciple of Confucius remarked, "A man who is a good son and a good citizen will seldom be found to be a man disposed to quarrel with those in authority over him; and men who are not disposed to quarrel with those in authority will never be found to disturb the peace and order of the State.

"A wise man devotes his attention to what is essential in the foundation of life. When the foundation is laid, wisdom will come. Now, to be a good son and a good citizen—do not these form the foundation of a moral life?"（辜鸿铭译）

（3）Few who respect their parents and their elders, said Master You, would do anything against their superiors. None who do nothing against their superiors would rise in revolt. An intelligentleman should be fundamentally good. A fundamentally good man will behave in the right way. Respect for one's parents and elder brothers is the fundamental quality for a good man.（许渊冲译）

（4）Youzi said, "It is a rare case that a man who has filial piety and fraternal love will be liable to offend his superior; it never occurs that a man who does not offend his superior will rebel. A superior man strives to establish his moral foundation, on which he forms his own principle. Filial piety and fraternal love are the foundation of benevolence."（吴国珍译）

此章是有子对孔子仁学的感悟，指出了行孝是仁的根本。

例2.
［原文］
曾子曰："慎终，追远，民德归厚矣。"（《论语》1/9）
［今译］
（1）曾子说："认真办理父母亲丧事，追怀、祭祀历代祖先，老百姓的品德就会忠实厚重。"（李泽厚译）
（2）曾子说："慎重地办好父母临终前后的大事，缅怀他们长远无尽的恩德，上位君子力行孝道，就能影响民间道德风尚回归淳厚了。"（天宜译）
［英译］
（1）The philosopher Tsǎng said, "Let there be a careful attention to perform the funeral rites to parents, and let them be followed when long gone with the ceremonies of sacrifice; —then the virtue of the people will resume its proper excellence."（理雅各译）

（2）A disciple of Confucius remarked, "By cultivating respect for the dead, and carrying the memory back to the distant past, the moral feeling of the people will waken and grow in depth."（辜鸿铭译）

（3）If a ruler regrets the death of his parents, said Master Zeng, and never forgets his ancestors, then people would follow him in doing good.（许渊冲译）

曾子是传承孔门儒学的杰出代表，这一章是曾子对孝道的最高体悟和完善总结，呼唤大同时代淳厚民风的回归。

"慎终，追远"在原文中没有主语，今译对其有不同的诠释，英译也有不同的翻译方式。

例3.

[原文]

孟懿子问孝。子曰："无违。"樊迟御，子告之曰："孟孙问孝于我，我对曰：'无违。'"

樊迟曰："何谓也？"子曰："生，事之以礼；死，葬之以礼，祭之以礼。"（《论语》2/5）

[今译]

孟懿子向孔子问孝道。孔子说："不要违背礼节。"不久，樊迟替孔子赶车，孔子便告诉他说："孟孙向我问孝道，我答复说，不要违背礼节。"樊迟道："这是什么意思？"孔子道："父母活着，依规定的礼节侍奉他们；死了，依规定的礼节埋葬他们，祭祀他们。"（杨伯峻译）

[英译]

（1）Măngî asked what filial piety was. The Master said, "It is not being disobedient." Soon after, as Fan Ch'ih was driving him, the Master told him, saying, "Măng-sun asked me what filial piety was, and I answered him, — 'not being disobedient.'"

Fan Ch'ih said, "What did you mean?" The Master replied, "That parents, when alive, should be served according to propriety; that, when dead, they should be buried according to propriety; and that they should be sacrificed to according to propriety." （理雅各译）

（2）A noble of the Court in Confucius' native State asked him what constituted the duty of a good son. Confucius answered, "Do not fail in what is required of you."

Afterwards, as a disciple was driving him in his carriage, Confucius told the disciple, saying, "My lord M— asked me what constituted the duty of a good son, and I answered, 'Do not fail in what is required of you.'"

"What did you mean by that?" asked the disciple.

"I meant," replied Confucius, "when his parents are living, a good son should do his duties to them according to the usage prescribed by propriety; when they are dead, he should bury them and honour their memory according to the rites prescribed by propriety." （辜鸿铭译）

（3）When Meng Yi Zi asked about filial duty, the Master said, "Do nothing in disagreement with the rites." When Fan Chi was driving his carriage for him, the Master told him how he answered the question of Meng Yi Zi. When Fan Chi asked for an explanation, the Master said, "Parents should be served in agreement with the rites while alive; when dead, they should be buried and the sacrifice be offered in agreement with the rites. "（许渊冲译）

[讨论]

分析"无违"在三个译文中的不同体现：

It is not being disobedient。

Do not fail in what is required of you.

Do nothing in disagreement with the rites.

例4.

[原文]

子游问孝。子曰："今之孝者，是谓能养①。至于犬马，皆能有养；不敬，何以别乎？"（《论语》2/7）

[今译]

（1）子游问如何是孝？孔子说："今天所谓孝只讲能够养活父母。人也一样养活狗、马。不尊敬，那有什么区别？"（李泽厚译）

（2）子游问孝道。孔子说："现在的所谓孝，就是说能够养活爹娘便行了。至于狗、马都能够得到饲养；若不存心严肃地孝顺父母，那养活爹娘和饲养狗、马怎样去分别呢？"（杨伯峻译）

[英译]

（1）Tsze-yû asked what filial piety was. The Master said, "The filial piety of nowadays means the support of one's parents. But dogs and horses likewise are able to do something in the way of support; —without reverence, what is there to distinguish the one support given from the other?"（理雅各译）

（2）A disciple of Confucius asked him the same question as the above. Confucius answered, "The duty of a good son nowadays means only to be able to support his parents. But you also keep your dogs and horses alive. If there is no feeling of love and respect, where is the difference?"（辜鸿铭译）

（3）When Zi You asked about filial duty, the Master said, "Filial sons of today only take care their parents are well fed. But even dogs and horses are well fed now. What is the difference if their parents are fed without reverence?"（许渊冲译）

（4）When Ziyou asked how to show filial piety, the Master said, "Nowadays filial piety simply means the feeding of one's parents. But since dogs and horses may also get

---

① 养：念 yàng。"养父母"的"养"从前人读第四声（杨伯峻，2006：15）。

fed, what is there to distinguish the two if one shows no respect while supporting the parents?"（吴国珍译）

"至于犬马，皆能有养"句有不同诠释。有学者译为："犬马也能养活人，人养活人，若不加以敬，便和犬马的养活人无所分别。"（杨伯峻，2006：15）

[讨论]

"今之孝者，是谓能养"的不同译法：

The filial piety of nowadays means the support of one's parents.

The duty of a good son nowadays means only to be able to support his parents.

Filial sons of today only take care their parents are well fed.

Nowadays filial piety simply means the feeding of one's parents.

"至于犬马，皆能有养"的不同译文：

Dogs and horses likewise are able to do something in the way of support.

You also keep your dogs and horses alive.

Even dogs and horses are well fed now.

Dogs and horses may also get fed.

从不同的译文分析译者对原文中的"能养""能有养"的不同理解和诠释。

例5.

[原文]

子夏问孝。子曰："色难。有事，弟子服其劳；有酒食，先生馔①：曾②是以为孝乎？"（《论语》2/8）

[今译]

（1）子夏问孝道。孔子道："儿子在父母前经常有愉悦的容色，是件难事。有事情，年轻人效劳；有酒有肴，年长的人吃喝，难道这竟可认为是孝吗？"（杨伯峻译）

（2）子夏向老师请教如何行孝。夫子说："难的是对父母要和颜悦色。如果只是有事情由儿女操劳，有酒与饭菜供父母食用，难道这样就算是孝了吗？"（天宜译）

[英译]

（1）Tsze-hsiâ asked what filial piety was. The Master said, "The difficulty is with the countenance. If, when their elders have any troublesome affairs, the young take the toil of them, and if when the young have wine and food, they set them before their elders, is THIS to be considered filial piety?"（理雅各译）

（2）Another disciple asked the same question. Confucius answered, "The difficulty

---

① 馔：念 zhuàn，意"饮食，吃喝"。

② 曾：念 zēng，意"竟也"。

is with the expression of your look. That merely when anything is to be done the young people do it, and when there is food and wine the old folk are allowed to enjoy it, do you think that is the whole duty of a good son?"（辜鸿铭译）

（3）When Zi Xia asked about filial duty, the Master said, "It is difficult to appear happy in trouble. If the young serve the old and feed them with wine and food before themselves, but with troubled looks, could they be call filial sons?"（许渊冲译）

（4）When Zixia asked how to show filial piety to parents, the Master said, "It is difficult to always show them your complaisant countenance. When necessary, the young may labor to wait on the elderly, and supply them with food and drink. But can that alone be counted as real filial piety?"（吴国珍译）

此篇孔子强调的是那颗对父母的实实在在的孝心，强调发自内心的真诚供奉优于劳力、酒食（天宜，2010：17）。

辜鸿铭的译文中增添"the whole duty"，更能确切表达原文中对"孝"中"色难"的强调。

许渊冲的译文中增添"but with troubled looks"，以便更确切地表述原文的意思。

［讨论］

对于原文中"色难"的翻译，哪位译者的翻译更确切，为什么？

例6.

［原文］

孟武伯问孝。子曰："父母唯其疾之忧。"（《论语》2/6）

［今译］

（1）孟武伯向孔子请教孝道。孔子道："做爹娘的只是为孝子的疾病发愁。"（杨伯峻译）

（2）孟武伯问："怎样是孝道？"先生说："使父母只担心子女的疾病。"（钱穆译）

（3）孟武伯问孔子如何做才算是孝子，孔子说："要让父母只对他们的生病感到担忧。"（吴国珍译）

［英译］

（1）Mǎng Wû asked what filial piety was. The Master said, "Parents are anxious lest their children should be sick. "（理雅各译）

（2）A son of the noble mentioned above put the same question to Confucius as his father did. Confucius answered, "Think how anxious your parents are when you are sick, and you will know your duty towards them. "（辜鸿铭译）

（3）When the son of Meng Yi Zi asked about filial duty, the Master said, "Do not let your parents worry about their health. "（许渊冲译）

（4）When Mengwubo asked how to be filial sons, the Master said, "Let the parents worry about nothing but their illness. "（吴国珍译）

对于此篇中"唯其疾之忧"的现代诠释，不同的学者有不同的见解。其一，父母爱子，无所不至，因此常忧其子之或病。子女能体此心，于日常生活加意谨慎，是即孝。其二，子女常以谨慎持身，使父母唯以其疾病为忧，言他无可忧。其三，子女诚心孝其父母，或用心过盛，转使父母不安，故为子女者，唯当以父母之疾病为忧，其他不宜过分操心（钱穆，2011：28）。

根据不同译者的译文，分析译者对原文的不同理解和诠释。

例 7.

[原文]

《话语》子曰："父在，观其志；父没①，观其行；三年②无改于父之道③，可谓孝矣。"（《论语》1/11）

[今译]

（1）孔子说："当他父亲活着，（因为他无权独立行动，）要观察他的志向；他父亲死了，要考察他的行为；若是他对他父亲的合理部分，长期地不加改变，可以说做到孝了。"（杨伯峻译）

（2）夫子说："看一个人，父亲在世时观察他的志向，父亲去世后观察他的行为。若能三年不改变父亲良好的家教家风，可说是尽孝了。"（天宜译）

[英译]

（1）The Master said, "While a man's father is alive, look at the bent of his will; when his father is dead, look at his conduct. If for three years he does not alter from the way of his father, he may be called filial. "（理雅各译）

（2）Confucius remarked, "When a man's father is living the son should have regard to what his father would have him do, when the father is dead, to what his father has done. A son who for three years after his father's death does not in his own life change his father's principles, may be said to be a good son. "（辜鸿铭译）

（3）Judge a man by what he will do to his father who is alive, said the Master, and by what he has done to his father who is dead. A son who does not alter his father's ways three years after the father's death may be called filial. （许渊冲译）

---

① 没：念 mò，通"殁"，死亡。

② 三年：古人的这种数字，有时泛指一段很长的时间。

③ 道：一般情况下是泛指名词，无论好坏善恶都可以叫作道，但更多时候是积极意义的名词，表示善的、好的东西（杨伯峻，2006：8）。

(4) The Master said, "We view a man by looking into his ideal while his father is still alive; when his father is dead, we watch his actions. If for three years he does not change his father's way, he may be counted as an obedient son. " (吴国珍译)

[讨论]

比较四位译者对于"三年无改于父之道"的译文，对原文意思的诠释是否有差异？

If the son for three years does not alter from the way of his father… (理雅各译)

A son who for three years after his father's death does not, in his own life, change his father's principles… (辜鸿铭译)

A son, who does not alter his father's ways three years after his death… (许渊冲译)

If for three years he does not change his father's way… (吴国珍译)

例8.

[原文]

子曰："事父母几①谏，见志不从，又敬不违，劳而不怨。"（《论语》4/18）

[今译]

孔子说："侍奉父母，如果发现他们有不对的地方，得轻微婉转地劝止，看到自己的心意没有被听从，仍然恭敬地不触犯他们，虽然忧愁，但不怨恨。"（杨伯峻译）

[英译]

(1) The Master said, "In serving his parents, a son may remonstrate with them, but gently; when he sees that they do not incline to follow his advice, he shows an increased degree of reverence, but does not abandon his purpose; and should they punish him, he does not allow himself to murmur. " (理雅各译)

(2) Confucius remarked, "In serving his parents a son should seldom remonstrate with them; but if he was obliged to do so, and should find that they will not listen, he should yet not fail in respect nor disregard their wishes; however much trouble they may give him, he should never complain. " (辜鸿铭译)

(3) In serving one's parents, said the Master, one may make remonstrance. If it is rejected, the son should show no discontent, but resume an attitude of deference and reiterate his remonstrance without complaint. (许渊冲译)

(4) The Master said, "In serving your parents, gently remonstrate with them when they are wrong. When seeing that they won't listen to you, respect them all the same rather than offend them, and show your anxiety rather than discontent. " (吴国珍译)

---

① 几：念 jī，表示委婉、婉转之意。

在此篇，孔子教导人们在父母有过失时应该如何与父母相处。父母有不对之处，一定要规劝，但态度必须要好，要有百折不挠的耐心（天宜，2010：58）。

例9.

[原文]

子曰："父母在，不远游，游必有方。"（《论语》4/19）

[今译]

（1）孔子说："父母在世，不出远门，如果出远门，必须有确定的去处。"（杨伯峻译）

（2）夫子说："父母健在，不出门到远方游历，若不得已而远出办事，也一定禀告明确的去向让父母放心。"（天宜译）

[英译]

（1）The Master said, "While his parents are alive, the son may not go abroad to a distance. If he does go abroad, he must have a fixed place to which he goes. "（理雅各译）

（2）Confucius remarked, "While his parents are living, a son should not go far abroad; if he does, he should let them know where he goes. "（辜鸿铭译）

（3）When father and mother are alive, said the Master, a good son should not go afar. If he does, they should be informed where he is going.（许渊冲译）

例10.

[原文]

子曰："父母之年，不可不知也：一则以喜，一则以惧。"（《论语》4/21）

[今译]

（1）孔子说："父母的年纪不能不时时记在心里：一方面因其高寿而喜欢，一方面又因其高寿而有所恐惧。"（杨伯峻译）

（2）夫子说："父母的年龄，不能不念念于心：一方面因为他们长寿而喜悦，一方面也因为他们年迈体衰而担心。"（天宜译）

[英译]

（1）The Master said, "The years of parents may by no means not be kept in the memory, as an occasion at once for joy and for fear. "（理雅各译）

（2）Confucius remarked, "A son should always keep in mind the age of his parents, as a matter for thankfulness as well as for anxiety. "（辜鸿铭译）

（3）The age of one's parents, said the Master, should not be forgotten. Old age may bring comfort on the one hand and worry on the other.（许渊冲译）

(4) The Master said, "Never forget your parents' ages. On the one hand, it is a cause for joy; on the other hand, it is a matter of concern. "（吴国珍译）

二、翻译练习与思考

（一）翻译练习：将下列句子翻译为英文

1. 君子务本，本立而道生。
2. 孝弟也者，其为仁之本与？
3. 今之孝者，是谓能养。
4. 三年无改于父之道。
5. 父母之年，不可不知也。

（二）思考与讨论

Recently, a hit show "All Is Well" （《都挺好》）, which premiered on March 1st, 2019 on provincial television, questions blind obedience to unreasonable parents. The show tells a story of a fictional Chinese family torn by internal conflicts. The female protagonist, Su Mingyu, is barely on speaking terms with her widowed father and one of her two brothers.

The father is a nagging crank who expects his two adult sons to bankroll his lavish tastes. This leads to constant bickering between the brothers, neither of whom wants to be called unfilial. (Taken from VOA Special English, 2019 - 04 - 02 China Television Drama)

So the questioning of blind attachment to traditional values in "All Is Well" is causing a stir. Many Chinese can relate to the Su family's troubles. The daughter holds a grudge against her father, and especially against her late mother, for having mistreated her while pampering her brothers.

… Some viewers have used social media to share their own tales of sexism within their family.

But the biggest reaction has been to the drama's critique of filial piety. Even today, the Confucian principles of unswerving loyalty to one's parents remain hallowed.

Many people say the best measure of adherence to this virtue is whether a son takes good care of his parents in old age.

… But it also reflects a culture of "never saying no to your parents", says an "All Is Well" fan in Beijing. Commentators on social media have taken to calling the father a *juying* ("giant baby"), a characteristic common among parents in real life, they say.

The Su children do their duty, but the audience is supposed to applaud the resentment they express.

Based on what you have learned about "filial piety" as said by Confucius, present your ideas concerning filial piety in modern China.

第六章 《论语》中关于"君子"的论述及其译文赏析

在孔子的时代，君子有两种含义，一指具有贵族血统且居于高位的政府官员，一指品德高尚的人。孔子在其私学施教的目标之一就是将其弟子培养成"君子"。孔子不仅要求其弟子具备他在《论语》中所提及的君子的品德，也要求他们日常的行为具有君子风范。

本章通过赏析《论语》原文及译文中关于"君子"的论述，探讨《论语》中"君子"的思想及其在英译文中的体现。

一、翻译实例与赏析

例1.

[原文]

子曰："君子不器。"（《论语》2/12）

[今译]

孔子说："君子不像器皿一般（只有一定的用途）。"（杨伯峻译）

[英译]

（1）The Master said，"The accomplished scholar is not an utensil."（理雅各译）

（2）Confucius remarked，"A wise man will not make himself into a mere machine fit only to do one kind of work."（辜鸿铭译）

（3）An intelligentleman，said the Master，is not a mere implement.（许渊冲译）

（4）The Master said，"A superior man is not a utensil."（吴国珍译）

对此篇的理解，不同学者有不同的见解。有学者认为，在此篇中孔子告诫弟子们，担任政府职务的人，不应该将自己当作一个器具，局限于琐碎的具体事务（吴国珍，2012：79）；也有学者认为，在此篇中孔子认为君子应该是无所不通的（杨伯峻，2006：18），而对此篇不同的理解也来自对于原文中"君子"的含义的不同理解。

[讨论]

不同译者对原文的"君子"采用了不同的译法，理雅各、辜鸿铭、许渊冲、吴国珍分别将"君子"译为：the accomplished scholar、a wise man、an intelligentleman、 a superior man。试根据不同译者的不同翻译讨论译者对"君子"内涵的不同理解。

例2.

[原文]

子曰:"君子不重,则不威;学则不固。主忠信。无友不如己者。过则勿惮改。"(《论语》1/8)

[今译]

孔子说:"君子,如果不庄重,就没有威严;即使读书,所学的也不会巩固。要以忠和信两种道德为主。不要跟不如自己的人交朋友。有了过错,就不要怕改正。"(杨伯峻译)

[英译]

(1) The Master said, "If the scholar be not grave, he will not call forth any veneration, and his learning will not be solid.

"Hold faithfulness and sincerity as first principles.

"Have no friends not equal to yourself.

"When you have fault, do not fear to abandon them." (理雅各译)

(2) Confucius remarked, "A wise man who is not serious will not inspire respect; what he learns will not remain permanent.

"Make conscientiousness and sincerity your first principles.

"Have no friends who are not as yourself. When you have bad habits do not hesitate to change them." (辜鸿铭译)

(3) An intelligentleman, said the Master, should not be frivolous, or he would lack solemnity in his behavior and solidity in his learning. He should be truthful and faithful, and befriend his equals. He should not be afraid of admitting and amending his faults. (许渊冲译)

(4) The Master said, "Without stately manners a superior man cannot stand on dignity, nor can he lay a solid learning foundation. He should hold the sense of loyalty and faithfulness as prime principle, and have no friends who are of lower levels. When he has faults, he should not be afraid to correct them." (吴国珍译)

此章体现了孔子对君子在修习仁学方面的要求,也体现了孔子对于弟子在自我修学以及交往之道等方面的观点。孔子要求其弟子既要看重敦厚、持重的外表,做学问也要扎实、牢固,与志同道合之人为伍,随时修正自己的错误,尽快提升自己。

[讨论]

在翻译实践中，为了使译文忠实而合乎语言习惯地传达原文的意思，有时必须把原文中的肯定说法变成译文中的否定说法，或把原文中的否定说法变成译文中的肯定说法。对于原文中的"无友不如己者"，几位译者的译文分别为：Have no friends not equal to yourself；Have no friends who are not as yourself；befriend his equals；have no friends who are of lower levels。

讨论四位译者对于原文中的反说所采取的不同的处理方式（反说反译及反说正译法）。

例3.

[原文]

子曰："质①胜文②则野③，文胜质则史④。文质彬彬⑤，然后君子。"（《论语》6/18）

[今译]

（1）孔子说："朴实多于文采，就未免粗野；文采多于朴实，又未免虚浮。文采和朴实，配合得当，这才是个君子。"（杨伯峻译）

（2）孔子说："质朴超过文采，就会流于粗俗；文采超过质朴，就会流于虚华。只有把内在的质朴和外在的文采恰当地结合起来，才能造就出君子。"（吴国珍译）

[英译]

（1）The Master said, "Where the solid qualities are in excess of accomplishments, we have rusticity; where the accomplishments are in excess of the solid qualities, we have the manners of a clerk. When the accomplishments and solid qualities are equally blended, we then have the man of complete virtue. "（理雅各译）

（2）Confucius remarked, "When the natural qualities of men get the better of the results of education, they are rude men. When the results of education get the better of their natural qualities, they become literati. It is only when the natural qualities and the results of education are properly blended, that we have the truly wise and good man. "（辜鸿铭译）

（3）More natural than cultured, said the Master, one would appear rustic. More cultured than natural, one would appear artificial. An intelligentleman should appear both

---

① 质：质朴。

② 文：文采。

③ 野：粗野。

④ 史：本义指衙门里的书记员，擅长写一些华而不实的文章。此处通常认为指虚饰、浮夸。

⑤ 彬彬：恰当地结合，文质兼备。

cultured and natural. （许渊冲译）

（4）The Master said, "When his plain nature prevails over his exterior brilliancy, a man appears coarse; when his exterior brilliancy outshines his plain nature, he appears flashy. The proper combination of exterior brilliancy with plain nature helps make a true superior man." （吴国珍译）

在此章，孔子指出君子应该同时具有内在的质朴和外在的文采。

吴国珍的译文里，译者将"君子"译为"superior man"，指的是具有贵族血统的身居高位的官员。当人们谈到"外在的文采"时，指的是拥有诸如文采、口才、高贵的衣着打扮等。孔子认为，君子不仅应该具有内在的质朴品质，还需要具有外在的文采。孔子培养其学生，希望其学生能够不断修习仁学，然后从政，实现其政治抱负。当他看到他的弟子大部分出身贫寒，拥有质朴的内心，不注重自己外在的文采时，他强调，作为君子，必须两者兼具（吴国珍，2012：186）。

例4.
［原文］
子曰："君子之于天下也，无适也，无莫也，① 义之与比②。"（《论语》4/10）
［今译］
（1）孔子说："君子对于天下的事情，没规定要怎样干，也没规定不要怎么样干，只要怎样干合理恰当，便怎样干。"（杨伯峻译）
（2）孔子说："君子对待天下各种事务，既不存心敌视，也不倾心羡慕，只以正当合理作为衡量标准。"（李泽厚译）
［英译］
（1）The Master said, "The superior man, in the world, does not set his mind either for any thing, or against any thing; what is right he will follow." （理雅各译）
（2）Confucius remarked, "A wise man in his judgment of the world, has no predilections nor prejudices; he is on the side of what is right." （辜鸿铭译）
（3）A cultured man, said the Master, does not set his heart for or against anything in the world. He only does what is right. （许渊冲译）
（4）The Master said, "To a superior man, there is nothing in the world that he ought to do or ought not to do. He just does what is righteous." （吴国珍译）

---

① 适、莫：这两字在今译中有不同诠释。有的解为"亲疏远近"，"无适无莫"即为"情无亲疏远近"。有的解为"敌对与羡慕"，"无适无莫"即为"无所为仇，无所欣羡"（杨伯峻，2006：41）。

② 比：bì，靠拢，适合。义之与比：使之适合"义"。

杨伯峻认为，此章孔子强调天下事无一定模式，只要坚持合乎义的目标，即可灵活权宜处之。

例5.
[原文]

子曰："君子义以为质，礼以行之，孙以出之，信以成之。君子哉！"（《论语》15/18）

[今译]

（1）孔子说："君子（对于事业），以合宜为原则，依礼节实行它，用谦逊的言语说出它，用诚实的态度完成它。真是位君子啊。"（杨伯峻译）

（2）夫子说："君子以义作为行事的根本，用礼仪来实行它，用谦逊的态度来表达它，靠诚信来成就它，这才是君子啊。"（天宜译）

[英译]

（1）The Master said, "The superior man in everything considers righteousness to be essential. He performs it according to the rules of propriety. He brings it forth in humility. He completes it with sincerity. This is indeed a superior man. "（理雅各译）

（2）Confucius remarked："A wise and good man makes right the substance of his being；he carries it out with judgment and good sense；he speaks it with modesty；and he attains it with sincerity：—such a man is a really good and wise man！"（辜鸿铭译）

（3）An intelligentleman, said the Master, thinks it his duty to do what is right, carries it out according to the rules of propriety, speaks with modesty and accomplishes it faithfully. Such is an intelligentleman.（许渊冲译）

（4）The Master said, "A superior man takes righteousness as the foundation for all. Guided by the rules of propriety he puts it into practice；in humility he speaks it out；with sincerity he fulfills it. Such is a superior man indeed. "（吴国珍译）

"义"是孔子推崇的重要品质之一，重要性仅次于"仁"，孔子说君子立身处世要以义为本质，同时配合礼仪、谦逊、诚信三者来完成。

例6.
[原文]

子曰："士志于道，而耻恶衣恶食者，未足与议也。"（《论语》4/9）

[今译]

（1）孔子说："读书人有志于真理，但又以自己吃粗粮、穿破衣为耻辱，这种人不值得同他商议了。"（杨伯峻译）

（2）夫子说："一个读书人已经立志行道救世，却又以衣衫破旧、饮食粗劣为

耻辱，是不值得同他谈论道的。"（天宜译）

[英译]

（1）The Master said，"A scholar，whose mind is set on truth，and who is ashamed of bad clothes and bad food，is not fit to be discoursed with."（理雅各译）

（2）Confucius remarked，"It is useless to speak to a gentleman who wants to give himself up to serious studies and who yet is ashamed because of his poor food or bad clothes."（辜鸿铭译）

（3）If an intellectual，said the Master，has made up his mind to find out the right way of life but feels ashamed of plain clothes and plain food，I do not think he is worth talking with.（许渊冲译）

（4）The Master said，"It is not worthwhile to talk about the truth with scholars who feel it a shame to live off bad clothes or bad food while pursuing the truth."（吴国珍译）

[讨论]

几位译者对原文"恶衣恶食"的不同译法，所实现的意义有何不同？

例7.

[原文]

曾子曰："可以托六尺①之孤，可以寄百里之命，临大节，而不可夺也——君子人与？君子人也。"（《论语》8/6）

[今译]

（1）曾子说："可以把幼小的孤儿和国家的命脉都交付给他，面临安危存亡的紧要关头，却不动摇屈服——这种人，是君子人吗？是君子人哩。"（杨伯峻译）

（2）曾子说："可以将年幼的君主托付给他，可以委托他代理国事，面临生死存亡的紧急关头而不动摇屈服，这样的人是君子吗？是君子啊。"（天宜译）

[英译]

（1）The philosopher Tsang said，"Suppose that there is an individual who can be entrusted with the charge of a young orphan prince，and can be commissioned with authority over a state of a hundred *le*，and whom no emergency however great can drive from his principles；—is such a man a superior man？He is a superior man indeed."（理雅各译）

（2）A disciple of Confucius remarked，"A man who could be depended upon when the life of an orphan prince，his master's child，is entrusted to his care，or the safety of a

_____

① 六尺：古代尺短，六尺约合今日一百三十八厘米，身长六尺的人还是小孩，一般指十五岁以下的人。

kingdom is confided to his charge — who will not, in any great emergency of life and death, betray his trust, —such a man I would call a gentleman; such a man I would call a perfect gentleman." (辜鸿铭译)

(3) Master Zeng said, "Is he not an intelligentleman who can be entrusted with a helpless orphan prince and the fate of a state, and who dare to face danger without fear? Yes, he is." (许渊冲译)

(4) Zengzi said, "If he can be entrusted with a minor orphan prince, if he can be commissioned with the reign of a state, if he will never waver at the critical moment of life and death, can he be called a superior man? Yes, he is a superior man." (吴国珍译)

［讨论］
通过四位译者对于"六尺之孤"的翻译，了解译者对原文的不同诠释。

例8.
［原文］
孔子曰："君子有三戒：少之时，血气未定，戒之在色；及其壮也，血气方刚，戒之在斗；及其老也，血气既衰，戒之在得。"（《论语》16/7）
［今译］
孔子说："君子有三件事情应该警惕戒备：年轻的时候，血气未定，便要警戒，莫迷恋女色；等到壮大了，血气正旺盛，便要警戒，莫好胜喜斗；等到年老了，血气已经衰弱，便要警戒，莫贪求无厌。"（杨伯峻译）
［英译］
(1) Confucius said, "There are three things which the superior man guards against. In youth, when the physical powers are not yet settled, he guards against lust. When he is strong, and the physical powers are full of vigour, he guards against quarrelsomeness. When he is old, and the animal powers are decayed, he guards against covetousness." (理雅各译)

(2) Confucius remarked, "There are three things which a man should beware of in the three stages of his life. In youth, when the constitution of his body is not yet formed, he should beware of lust. In manhood, when his physical powers are in full vigour, he should beware of strife. In old age, when the physical powers are in decay, he should beware of greed." (辜鸿铭译)

(3) A cultured man, said Confucius, should beware of three things. He should beware of lust in youth when his vigor is uncouth, of strife in his prime when he is full of vigor, and of greed in old age when his vigor is on the decline. (许渊冲译)

增译法是为了准确表达原文的意思，在译文中增添词语，以表达原文作者在原文中省略的意思；或者译者把根据上下文理解的原文意思在译文中表述出来，使译文更符合译文读者的阅读习惯和理解需求。

[讨论]

讨论辜鸿铭的译文是否使用了增译法。与其他译文相比，其译文有何特点？

例9.

[原文]

子曰："君子固穷，小人穷斯滥矣。"（《论语》15/2）

[今译]

（1）孔子说："君子虽然穷困，仍能固守着道，小人一穷困就胡作非为了。"（天宜译）

（2）孔子说："君子走投无路时，仍然坚持原则；换了是小人，就胡作非为了。"（杨志英译）

（3）孔子道："君子虽然穷，还是坚持着，小人一穷便无所不为了。"（杨伯峻 译）。

[英译]

（1）The Master said, "The superior man may indeed have to endure want, but the mean man, when he is in want, gives way to unbridled license."（理雅各译）

（2）"Yes", replied Confucius, "a wise and good man sometimes also meets with distress; but a fool when in distress, becomes reckless."（辜鸿铭译）

（3）The Master said, "An intelligentleman will do nothing wrong even if he is in want, while an uncultured man in want will break loose from all restraints."（许渊冲译）

不同译者对于"君子固穷，小人穷斯滥矣"有不同译法。译者对于"穷"的理解，又有何不同呢？

The superior man may indeed have to endure want, but the mean man, when he is in want, gives way to unbridled license.（理雅各译）

A gentleman can withstand hardships; it is only the small man who, when submitted to them, is swept off his feet.（威利译）

A wise and good man sometimes also meets with distress; but a fool when in distress, becomes reckless.（辜鸿铭译）

An intelligentleman will do nothing wrong even if he is in want, while an uncultured man in want will break loose from all restraints.（许渊冲译）

理雅各和许渊冲的译文中，用"want"表示"穷"，认为君子应该忍受贫穷，安贫乐道，贪图物质享受就不是君子了。但也有学者认为，孔子说这句话时正从卫国逃难到陈国，"在陈绝粮，从者病"。这时子路很不高兴，颇有怨言，对孔子说：

"正人君子，也有穷途末路的时候吗?"孔子的回答就是上述这句话，意思是，"君子在没有办法的时候，仍然坚持着，普通的人没办法就胡来了"（李泽厚，2004：286）。显然，"穷"在这里并不仅仅局限于经济方面，而且还包括人生道路上遭遇挫折、事业坎坷。君子到了穷途末路还能固守其志，不屈膝变节、苟且偷生，体现了儒家思想对君子提倡的"崇高品质"。对这句话的翻译，威利和辜鸿铭的译文相对来说更接近这种对"穷"的理解（谢艳明，2019）。

例10.

[原文]

子夏曰："君子有三变：望之俨然，即之也温，听其言也厉。"（《论语》19/9）

[今译]

（1）子夏说："君子有三变：远远望着，庄严可畏；向他靠拢，温和可亲；听他的话，严厉不苟。"（杨伯峻译）

（2）子夏说："君子有三种变相：远望他庄严可畏，接近他温和可亲，听他讲话则准确犀利。"（天宜译）

[英译]

（1）Tsze-hsià said, "The superior man undergoes three changes. Looked at from a distance, he appears stern; when approached, he is mild; when he is heard to speak, his language is firm and decided. "（理雅各译）

（2）The same disciple remarked, "A good and wise man appears different from three points of view. When you look at him from a distance he appears severe; when you approach him he is gracious; when you hear him speak, he is serious. "（辜鸿铭译）

（3）Zi Xia said, "An intelligentleman has three different aspects：when seen from afar, he looks grave; when approached, he looks affable; when listened to, he looks dignified. "（许渊冲译）

（4）Zixia said, "A superior man presents different looks on these occasions：when viewed from a distance, he appears stern; when approached, he looks mild; when heard to speak, he sounds serious. "（吴国珍译）

此章是子夏对孔子仪度风范的描述。孔子集威严、恭敬、安详于一身，同时，言辞犀利准确，体现了孔子的智慧和才能（天宜，2010：329）。

例11.

[原文]

子曰："君子病无能焉，不病人之不己知也。"（《论语》15/19）

[今译] 孔子说："君子只惭愧自己没有能力，不怨恨别人不知道自己。"（杨

伯峻译）

[英译]

（1）Confucius remarked："A wise and good man should be distressed that he has no ability；he should never be distressed that men do not take notice of him."（辜鸿铭译）

（2）An intelligentleman，said the Master，regrets that he is incapable，and not that he is unknown.（许渊冲译）

（3）The Master said，"A man of virtue worries that he might lack abilities. He does not worry that others might not know about him."（吴国珍译）

例12.

[原文]

子曰："君子疾没世而名不称焉。"（《论语》15/20）

[今译]

（1）孔子说："到死而名声不被人家称述，君子引以为恨。"（杨伯峻译）

（2）孔子说："君子憎恶这个黑暗世界，名称不符合实际。"（李泽厚译）

[英译]

（1）The Master said，"The superior man dislikes the thought of his name not being mentioned after his death."（理雅各译）

（2）Confucius remarked："A wise and good man hates to die without having done anything to distinguish himself."（辜鸿铭译）

（3）The Master said，"A man of virtue worries that he may end up with no reputation."（吴国珍译）

（4）An intelligentleman，said the Master，dislikes the age of decadence when names belie facts.（许渊冲译）

对于此章，今译异解纷纭。有的学者说，"君子"也好名，尤其是"身后之名"；但有的学者认为，这种解释与《论语》15/19 所言的"君子病无能焉，不病人之不己知也"相矛盾。

二、翻译练习与思考

（一）翻译练习：将下列句子和词语翻译为英文

1. 君子不器。

2. 无友不如己。

3. 文质彬彬。

4. 君子固穷，小人穷斯滥矣。

5. 君子疾没世而名不称焉。

6. 士志于道，而耻恶衣恶食者，未足与议也。

7. 君子不重，则不威；学则不固。

8. 君子病无能焉，不病人之不己知也。

（二）思考与讨论

在本章例 12 对《论语》原文的翻译中，许渊冲的翻译与其他译者有何不同，表达的意义有何差异？

第七章 《论语》中关于"君子"与"小人"的论述及其译文赏析

孔子作为中国文化的先知，为中国社会两千多年的发展提供了影响深远的道德思想体系，为人的社会行为创设了崇高的德行标准。这一点主要体现在他对"君子"和"小人"的德操主张上。《论语》中提及"君子"107处，提及"小人"24处。《论语》把"君子"规约为一个德行高尚且受过良好教育、有一定的社会地位、具备高于常人的社会能力的道德楷模；"小人"常常和"君子"同时出现，但并不一定与"君子"的高尚德操相反，通常是指地位不高、格局不大的平民百姓或仆人，与道德品质无关。

由于在英语中找不到与原文"君子"和"小人"完全对等的词，这两个词的翻译，颇让译者绞尽脑汁，因而，不同的译者将其译成不同的词。本章探讨《论语》中关于"君子"与"小人"的论述及不同译者对其所做的诠释与翻译。

一、翻译实例与赏析

例1.

[原文]

子曰："君子喻于义，小人喻于利。"（《论语》4/16）

[今译]

（1）孔子说："君子懂得的是义，小人懂得的是利"。（杨伯峻译）

（2）夫子说："君子明白义，小民只懂得利。"（天宜译）

[英译]

（1）The Master said, "The mind of the superior man is conversant with righteousness; the mind of the mean man is conversant with gain."（理雅各译）

（2）Confucius remarked, "A wise man sees what is right in a question; a fool, what is advantageous to himself."（辜鸿铭译）

（3）A cultured man cares for what is proper and fit while an uncultured man cares for the profit.（许渊冲译）

（4）The Master said, "A man of virtue is penetrable to reason; a base man can only be persuaded with benefits."（吴国珍译）

杨伯峻（2006：43）认为，"君子"是指在位者，还是指有德者，还是两者兼指，孔子原意不得而知。天宜（2010：52）认为，此处君子指的是在位者，小人指的是普通民众，孔子在此告诉弟子们，当官为政的根本目标之一是行道教化民众，当安在仁义，行在仁义，境界无疑在百姓之上。在孔子的心里，义是一把衡量君子与小人的尺子。

从吴国珍的译文可以看出，译者认为，孔子此处指出，当要说服一个君子的时候，你只需以礼义告知，而当你要说服一个小人的时候，你必须诱之以利（吴国珍，2012：131）。

例2.

[原文]

子曰："君子怀德，小人怀土；君子怀刑，小人怀惠。"（《论语》4/11）

[今译]

（1）孔子说："君子怀念道德，小人怀念乡土；君子关心法度，小人关心恩惠。"（杨伯峻译）

（2）夫子说："君子念念不忘道德，小人念念不忘乡土，君子关心法制，小人关心恩惠。"（天宜译）

（3）孔子说："君子时时不忘坚守品德，小人念念不忘安居乐土；君子时时牢记法律制度，小人念念不忘谋取利益。"（吴国珍译）

[英译]

（1）The Master said, "The superior man thinks of virtue; the small man thinks of comfort. The superior man thinks of the sanctions of law; the small man thinks of favors which he may receive. "（理雅各）

（2）Confucius remarked, "A wise man regards the moral worth of a man; a fool, only his position. A wise man expects justice; a fool, only expects favors. "（辜鸿铭译）

（3）A cultured man cares for virtue, said the Master, and an uncultured man for the land. The former cares for order and the latter for favor.（许渊冲译）

（4）The Master said, "A superior man holds to morality, while a petty man clings to his lotus land. A superior man holds to legal laws, while a petty man clings to his benefits. "（吴国珍译）

天宜认为，孔子在此篇教导弟子在布仁行道时要有知人之明，善于区分君子、小人人生志向的不同（天宜，2010：50）。

例3.

[原文]

子曰："君子周而不比①，小人比而不周。"（《论语》2/14）

[今译]

（1）孔子说："君子是团结，而不是勾结；小人是勾结，而不是团结。"（杨伯峻译）

（2）夫子说："君子广泛地团结人而不结党营私，小人结党营私而不能广泛地团结人。"（天宜译）

[英译]

（1）The Master said, "The superior man is catholic and no partizan. The mean man is a partizan and not catholic. "（理雅各译）

（2）Confucius remarked, "A wise man is impartial, not neutral. A fool is neutral but not impartial. "（辜鸿铭译）

（3）An intelligentleman, said the Master, cares for the whole more than for the parts, while an uncultured man cares for the parts rather than for the whole. （许渊冲译）

（4）The Master said, "The virtuous people widely unite but not gang up; the virtuous people gang up but not widely unite. "（吴国珍译）

杨伯峻（2010：18）认为，"周"指用道义来团结人，"比"指以暂时共同利益互相勾结。

天宜则认为，此篇孔子教导弟子，君子治理天下，应以天下事国事为重，不要结党营私，也不要让小人投机所好，钻了空子，坏了规矩（天宜，2010：20）。

注意理雅各译文所选词语 catholic 及 partizan 的含义。

例4.

[原文]

子曰："君子和而不同，小人同而不和。"（《论语》13/23）

[今译]

（1）孔子说："君子和谐却不同一，小人同一却不和谐。"（李泽厚译）

（2）孔子说："君子和谐相处而不盲目附和，小人盲目附和而不和谐相处。"（吴国珍译）

[英译]

（1）The Master said, "The superior man is affable, but not adulatory; the mean man is adulatory, but not affable. "（理雅各译）

---

① 比，旧读 bì，勾结。

（2）Confucius remarked: "A wise man is sociable, but not familiar. A fool is familiar but not sociable." （辜鸿铭译）

（3）A cultured man, said the Master, may disagree to reach an agreement, while an uncultured man dare not disagree but agrees without understanding. （许渊冲译）

（4）The Master said, "The superior men harmonize without demanding conformity; the base men demand conformity but not harmonize." （吴国珍译）

李泽厚（2004：370）认为，孔子在此篇告诫弟子，只有保持个体的特殊性和独立性才有社会和人际的和谐，强求一致，没有好结果，多极、多元才能发展。

[讨论]

几位译者对原文的诠释各有不同，哪位译者的译文更能确切地表达原文的意思？理雅各译文中的 affable 和 adulatory 是否能准确表达原文的意思？

例5.

[原文]

子曰："君子矜而不争，群而不党。"（《论语》15/22）

[今译]

（1）孔子说："君子庄矜而不争执，合群而不闹宗派。"（杨伯峻译）

（2）孔子说："君子庄重而与人无争，合群而不结党营私。"（吴国珍译）

[英译]

（1）The Master said, "The superior man is dignified, but does not wrangle. He is sociable, but not a partisan." （理雅各译）

（2）Confucius remarked, "A wise man is proud but not vain; he is sociable, but belongs to no party." （辜鸿铭译）

（3）The Master said, "Men of virtue are dignified, but do not contend against each other. They are sociable, but do not gang up." （吴国珍译）

（4）An intelligentleman, said the Master, is dignified, but not quarrelsome; he is sociable, but not partisan. （许渊冲译）

"群而不党"可能包含着"周而不比"以及"和而不同"两个意思（杨伯峻，2010：188）。

[讨论]

理雅各译文中，dignified, wrangle, sociable 和 partisan 的内涵是什么？

辜鸿铭译文中的 vain，是否能准确表达原文的内涵？

例6.

[原文]

子曰:"君子坦荡荡,小人长戚戚。"(《论语》7/37)

[今译]

夫子说:"君子心胸平坦宽广,小人经常忧愁不安。"(天宜译)

[英译]

(1) The Master said, "The superior man is satisfied and composed; the mean man is always full of distress. "(理雅各译)

(2) Confucius remarked, "A wise and good man is composed and happy; a fool is always worried and full of distress. "(辜鸿铭译)

(3) An intelligentleman, said the Master, is carefree while an uncultured man is careworn. (许渊冲译)

(4) The Master said, "A gentleman is open and broad-hearted; a base man is always worried and sorrowed. "(吴国珍译)

在此篇中,孔子强调君子与小人不同的处事态度。君子遵行的是天理,所以安宁舒畅;小人常被外物所困,常常忧伤悲戚(天宜,2010:115)。

[讨论]

许渊冲译文中选择 carefree 和 careworn 来表示原文的"坦荡荡"与"长戚戚",与其他译文相比有何特点?

例7.

[原文]

子曰:"君子成人之美,不成人之恶。小人反是。"(《论语》12/16)

[今译]

夫子说:"君子促成人家的好事,而不帮助别人做坏事。小人恰恰相反。"(天宜译)

[英译]

(1) The Master said, "The superior man seeks to perfect the admirable qualities of men, and does not seek to perfect their bad qualities. The mean man does the opposite of this. "(理雅各译)

(2) Confucius remarked, "a good and wise man encourages men to develop the good qualities in their nature, and not their bad qualities; whereas, a bad man and a fool does the very opposite. "(辜鸿铭译)

(3) A cultured man, said the Master, will help others in doing good, not in doing wrong. An uncultured man will do the contrary. (许渊冲译)

例8.

[原文]

子曰："君子不以言举人，不以人废言。"（《论语》15/23）

[今译]

孔子说："君子不因为人家一句话（说得好）便提拔他，不因为他是坏人而鄙弃他的好话。"（杨伯峻译）

[英译]

（1）The Master said，"The superior man does not promote a man simply on account of his words，nor does he put aside good words because of the man."（理雅各译）

（2）Confucius remarked，"A wise man never upholds a man because of what he says，nor does he discard what a man says because of the speaker's character."（辜鸿铭译）

（3）An intelligentleman，said the Master，will not recommend anyone simply because of his good words，nor reject the good words of anyone.（许渊冲译）

例9.

[原文]

子曰："君子上达，小人下达。"（《论语》14/23）

[今译]

（1）孔子说："君子通达于仁义，小人通达于财利。"（杨伯峻译）

（2）夫子说："君子向上，通达仁义，小人向下，达到财利。"（天宜译）

（3）孔子说："君子向上追求道义，小人向下寻求实利。"（吴国珍译）

[英译]

（1）The Master said，"The progress of the superior man is upwards；the progress of the mean man is downwards."（理雅各译）

（2）Confucius remarked，"A wise and good man looks upwards in his aspiration；a fool look downwards."（辜鸿铭译）

（3）A cultured man，said the Master，goes up while an uncultured man goes down.（许渊冲译）

（4）The Master said，"A superior man aims high，while an ordinary man directs downward."（吴国珍译）

孔子认为，君子与小人最根本的差别是义（上达）与利（下达）的差别，向上走追求美善，实现生命价值，向下走追求绝对利益（杨志英，2013：85）。在辜鸿铭的译文中，aspiration 表示 a strong desire to have or achieve something，属于增译。

例10.

[原文]

子曰："君子求诸己，小人求诸人。"（《论语》15/21）

[今译]

（1）孔子说："君子要求自己，小人要求别人。"（杨伯峻译）

（2）夫子说："君子责求自己，小人责求他人。"（天宜译）

[英译]

（1）The Master said, "What the superior man seeks, is in himself. What the mean man seeks, is in others."（理雅各译）

（2）Confucius remarked："A wise man seeks for what he wants in himself; a fool seeks for it from others."（辜鸿铭译）

（3）An intelligentleman, said the Master, relies on himself while an uncultured man relies on others.（许渊冲译）

（4）The Master said, "A virtuous man finds faults with himself while a base man finds faults with others."（吴国珍译）

例11.

[原文]

子曰："君子泰而不骄，小人骄而不泰。"（《论语》13/26）

[今译]

（1）孔子说："君子安详舒泰，却不骄傲凌人；小人骄傲凌人，却不安详舒泰。"（杨伯峻译）

（2）夫子说："君子舒泰而不骄横，小人骄横而不舒泰。"（天宜译）

[英译]

（1）The Master said, "The superior man has a dignified ease without pride. The mean man has pride without a dignified ease."（理雅各译）

（2）Confucius remarked, "A wise man is dignified, but not proud. A fool is proud, but not dignified."（辜鸿铭译）

（3）A cultured man, said the Master, is dignified and not proud, while an uncultured man is proud and not dignified.（许渊冲译）

例12.

[原文]

子曰："君子不可小知，而可大受也；小人不可大受，而可小知也。"（《论语》15/34）

[今译]

（1）孔子道："君子不可以用小事情考验他，却可以接受重大任务；小人不可以接受重大任务，却可以用小事情考验他。"（杨伯峻译）

（2）夫子说："君子不能从小事上去度量，却可以担当重任。小人不能担当大任，却能担当小事。"（天宜译）

（3）孔子说："君子没有小聪明，却可以承担大任务。小人不能承担大任务，却可以有小聪明。"（李泽厚译）

[英译]

（1）The Master said, "The superior man cannot be known in little matters; but he may be intrusted with great concerns. The small men may not be intrusted with great concerns, but he may be known in little matters. "（理雅各译）

（2）Confucius remarked, "A wise and good man may not show his quality in small affairs, but he can be entrusted with great concerns. A fool may gain distinction in small things, but he cannot be entrusted with great concerns. "（辜鸿铭译）

（3）An intelligentleman, said the Master, may not know minor matters, but he can be entrusted with major duties. An uncultured man cannot be entrusted with major duties, but he may know minor matters.（许渊冲译）

在此篇中，天宜认为孔子主要告知弟子们知人用人的学问。而李泽厚认为，在此篇中，孔子主要告诫弟子们，人各有优点和缺点，不能求全责备。

例 13.

[原文]

孔子曰："君子有三畏：畏天命，畏大人，畏圣人之言。小人不知天命而不畏也，狎大人，侮圣人之言。"（《论语》16/8）

[今译]

孔子说："君子有三种惧怕：怕天命，怕王公大人，怕圣人讲的话。小人不懂天命，所以不怕，轻视大人，嘲笑圣人讲的话。"（李泽厚译）

[英译]

（1）The Master said, "There are three things of which the superior man stands in awe. He stands in awe of the ordinance of Heaven. He stands in awe of great men. He stands in awe of the words of sages.

"The mean man does not know the ordinances of Heaven, and consequently does not stand in awe of them. He is disrespectful to great men. He makes sport of the words of sages. "（理雅各译）

（2）Confucius remarked："There are three things which a wise and good man holds in awe. He holds in awe the Laws of God, persons in authority, and the words of wisdom of holy men. A fool, on the other hand, does not know that there are Laws of God；he, therefore, has no reverence for them；he is disrespectful to persons in authority, and contemns the words of wisdom of holy men. "（辜鸿铭译）

（3）Three things, said Confucius, inspire a cultured man with awe：Heaven's will, great men and words of the sage. An uncultured man does not know Heaven's will, so he does not stand in awe. He respects no great man, and makes light of the sage's words. （许渊冲译）

例 14.
[原文]
子贡曰："君子之过也，如日月之食焉。过也，人皆见之；更也，人皆仰之。"（《论语》19/21）

[今译]
（1）子贡说："君子的过失好比日蚀月蚀：错误的时候，每个人都看得见；更改的时候，每个人都仰望着。"（杨伯峻译）

（2）子贡说："君子的过错，如同日食月食一般朗朗呈现于天空。他犯了过错，人们都看得见；他更改过错，人们都仰望着他。"（天宜译）

[英译]
（1）Tsze-kung said, "The faults of the superior man are like the eclipses of the sun and moon. He has his faults, and all men see them；he changes again, and all men look up to him. "（理雅各译）

（2）The same disciple remarked, "The failings of a great man are eclipses of the sun and moon. When he fails, all men see it；but, when he recovers from his failing, all men look up to him as before. "（辜鸿铭译）

（3）Master Zeng said, "The faults of an intelligentleman are like eclipses of the sun or the moon. When he does something wrong, all men can see it. When he has amended his fault, all men look up to him. "（许渊冲译）

在此篇中，子贡认为君子不仅不掩盖过错，而且还要勇于公开改正错误，所以众人仍然仰慕他。

例 15.
[原文]
子夏曰："小人之过也，必文。"（《论语》19/8）

［今译］

子夏说："小人对于错误一定加以掩饰。"（杨伯峻译）

［英译］

（1）Tsze-hsià said，"The mean man is sure to gloss his faults."（理雅各译）

（2）The same disciple remarked，"A fool always has an excuse ready when he does wrong."（辜鸿铭译）

（3）Zi Xia said，"An uncultured man would certainly gloss his faults."（许渊冲译）

二、翻译练习与思考

（一）翻译练习：将下列句子和词组翻译为英文

1. 见贤思齐。
2. 吾日三省吾身。
3. 三军可夺帅也，匹夫不可夺志也。
4. 小人之过也，必文。
5. 君子坦荡荡，小人长戚戚。
6. 君子求诸己，小人求诸人。
7. 君子成人之美。
8. 君子泰而不骄，小人骄而不泰。
9. 君子上达，小人下达。
10. 君子和而不同，小人同而不和。

（二）思考与讨论

在《论语》的各种版本译文中，不同译者对原文的"君子"和"小人"采用了不同的英文词汇来体现。根据相关研究，理雅各将"君子"翻译成 20 种译文，译得最多的是 superior man，多达 83 次；其次是 man of complete virtue、man of superior virtue 和 the person in authority，各两次。余下 16 种各一次，分别为：scholar、accomplished scholar、student of virtue、chun-tsze、virtuous man、man of virtue、man of real talent and virtue、those who are in high stations、man of high rank、accomplished gentleman、superior、man of virtue and station、man of high station、man in a superior situation、virtuous prince 和 wise man。"小人"的译法有 8 种，其中，14 次译成 mean man，4 次译成 small man，余下各 1 次，分别为：inferior、little man、man of low station、small mean people、lower people、servant。

威利所译的"君子"，形式较少，全都译成了 gentleman，只是在一些地方加了修饰语 true 和 real；而他所译的"小人"，形式则多得多，共 10 种，其中 10 次

small man，4 次 common people，3 次 commoner，其余各 1 次，分别为：lesser man、small people、no gentleman、the humble、not a gentleman、man from low walks of life、people of low birth。

辜鸿铭将"君子"在不同的地方译成不同的形式，多达 12 种，其中 wise and good man 或 good and wise man 共 52 次，wise man 25 次，gentleman 14 次，good man 2 次，the ruler 2 次，其余各 2 次，包括 perfect gentleman、polite、superior、a man、scholar、great man、educated man。他将"小人"译成 fool（16 次）、the people（2 次）、bad man and fool（1 次）、petty-minded man（1 次）、small mean people（1 次）、man of the people（1 次）、servant（1 次）。

许渊冲译的"君子"也有 8 种形式，其中，他用自己造的词 intelligentleman 39 次，cultured man 40 次，余下各 1 次，包括 man of renown、man、the higher class、good man、the ruler、good ruler。他将"小人"译成 6 种形式，其中 uncultured man 有 15 次，余下各 1 次，包括 the lower class、townsfolk、the ruled、common people of lower class、servant 等。

由于"君子"是《论语》对人的德行进行规约的标杆，代表着崇高的文化品格，所以译者在选词时很慎重。理雅各主要选择的是 superior man，意思是"一个阶层、社会地位较高、个人品格高尚的人"，基本上涵盖了儒家"君子"的内涵，但有等级观念之嫌。威利主要选择 gentleman，这个词源自 gentry，是英国中世纪的"士绅阶层"，具有一定的社会地位。英国绅士十分注重自身的修养，他们彬彬有礼、待人谦和、衣冠得体、谈吐高雅、知识渊博、有爱心、尊老爱幼、尊重女性、无不良嗜好，是心地善良、举止优雅的男士。辜鸿铭主要选择的是 wise and good man；他关注"君子"的"聪明"和"善良"，淡化了"君子"的优良品德。许渊冲主要选择的是 cultured man 和 intelligentleman，注重"君子"的"教养"和"智慧"，也淡化了"君子"的品德。

"君子"的翻译其实不算最难的，倒是"小人"的翻译必须慎之又慎。

比如，《论语》13/4 记载：

樊迟请学稼。子曰："吾不如老农。"请学为圃。曰："吾不如老圃。"

樊迟出。子曰："小人哉，樊须也！上好礼，则民莫敢不敬；上好义，则民莫敢不服；上好信，则民莫敢不用情。夫如是，则四方之民襁负其子而至矣，焉用稼？"

在译文中，理雅各将"小人"译成"small man"；威利将"小人"与"君子"对举，译为"commoners""no gentleman"；辜鸿铭将其译为"a petty-minded man"；许渊冲将其译为"an uncultured man"。以上几个译本，哪个译本对于"小人"的翻译最为恰当？为什么？

练习答案

第一章

（一）将下列英文书名和标题翻译为中文

1.《诗经》
2.《论语》
3.《战国策》
4.《孟子》
5.《史记》
6.《庄子》
7.《桃花源记》
8.《三国志》

（二）将下面的英文翻译为中文

1. 劳心者治人，劳力者治于人。
2. 忠言逆耳利于行，良药苦口利于病。
3. 天时不如地利，地利不如人和。
4. 先天下之忧而忧，后天下之乐而乐。
5. 三思而后行。
6. 学而不厌，诲人不倦。

第二章

将下列句子翻译成英文

1. The Master said，"The commander of the forces of a large state may be carried

off, but the will of even a common man cannot be taken from him. "

2. The superior man is satisfied and composed; the mean man is always full of distress.

3. The mechanic, who wished to do his work well, must first sharpen his tools.

4. When I walk along with two others, they may serve me as my teachers. I will select their good qualities and follow them, their bad qualities and avoid them.

5. If a man keeps cherishing his old knowledge, so as continually to be acquiring the new, he may be a teacher of others.

6. The superior man does not promote a man simply on account of his words, nor does he put aside good words because of the man.

7. What you do not want done to yourself, do not do to others.

8. Have no friends not equal to yourself.

9. Youths should be respected.

10. While his parents are living, a son should not go far abroad; if he does, he should let them know where he goes.

第三章

（一）将下列句子翻译成英文

1. Is it not pleasant to learn with a constant perseverance and application?

2. If a man keeps cherishing his old knowledge, so as continually to be acquiring new, he may be a teacher of others.

3. Learning without thought is labour lost; thought without learning is perilous.

4. When you know a thing, to hold that you know it; and when you do not know a thing, to allow that you do not know it; —this is knowledge.

5. When three men meet together, one of them who is anxious to learn can always learn something of the other two.

6. He can profit by the good example of the one and avoid the bad example of the other.

7. Standing by a stream, the Master said, "Time passes away night and day like running water. "

8. Once, said the Master, I spent a whole day and a whole night in thinking, without eating and sleeping. I got no result and found it better to learn.

9. Zi Xia said, " If a man knows what he has not yet learned every day and does not

forget what he has learned every month, he may be said to be a lover of knowledge. "

10. The Master said, "The silent treasuring up of knowledge; learning without satiety; and instructing others without being wearied; — what one of these things belongs to me?"

(二) 思考与讨论

略

第四章

(一) 翻译练习：将下列句子和词组翻译为英文

1. (1) His burden is heavy and his course is long.

(2) His responsibility in life is a heavy one, and the way is long.

(3) His duty is heavy and his journey will be long.

2. (1) Let every man consider virtue as what devolves on himself. He may not yield the performance of it even to his teacher.

(2) When the question is one of morality, a man need not defer to his teacher.

(3) A good man, said the Master, should not withdraw from being a better man than his teacher.

3. (1) fine words and an insinuating appearance

(2) plausible speech and fine manners

(3) say what he does not believe, or pretend to appear better than he is

4. (1) It is virtuous manners which constitute the excellence of a neighbourhood.

(2) It is the moral life of a neighbourhood which constitutes its excellence.

(3) Good neighborhood, said the Master, adds beauty to life.

5. (1) The mechanic, who wished to do his work well, must first sharpen his tools.

(2) A workman who wants to perfect his work first sharpens his tools.

(3) A craftsman who wishes to do his work well must first sharpen his tools.

6. (1) Look not at what is contrary to propriety; listen not to what is contrary to propriety; speak not what is contrary to propriety; make no movement which is contrary to propriety.

(2) Whatever things are contrary to the ideal of decency and good sense, do not look upon them. Whatever things are contrary to the ideal of decency and good sense, do

not listen to them. Whatever things are contrary to the ideal of decency and good sense, do not utter them with your mouth. Lastly, let nothing in whatever things you do, act or move, be contrary to the ideal of decency and good sense.

(3) Do not look at anything nor listen to anything nor speak of anything nor do anything against the rules of propriety.

7. (1) The wise find pleasure in water; the virtuous find pleasure in hills.

(2) Men of intellectual character delight in water scenery; men of moral character delight in mountain scenery.

(3) The wise, said the Master, delight in water while the good delight in mountains.

8. (1) The wise are active; the virtuous are tranquil.

(2) Intellectual men are active; moral men are calm.

(3) The wise love mobility while the good love tranquility.

9. (1) The wise are joyful, the virtuous are long-lived.

(2) Intellectual men enjoy life; moral men live long.

(3) The wise live happy while the good live long.

10. The man of virtue makes the difficulty to be overcome his first business, and success only a subsequent consideration.

(二) 思考与讨论

略

第五章

(一) 翻译练习: 将下列句子翻译为英文

1. (1) The superior man bends his attention to what is radical. That being established, all practical courses naturally grow up.

(2) A wise man devotes his attention to what is essential in the foundation of life. When the foundation is laid, wisdom will come.

(3) An intelligentleman should be fundamentally good. A fundamentally good man will behave in the right way.

2. (1) Filial piety and fraternal submission! —Are they not the root of all benevolent actions?

(2) To be a good son and a good citizen—do not these form the foundation of a moral

life?

（3） Respect for one's parents and elder brothers is the fundamental quality for a good man.

3. The filial piety of nowadays means the support of one's parents.

4. A son for three years after his father's death does not, in his own life, change his father's principles.

5. The years of parents may by no means not be kept in the memory.

（二） 思考与讨论

略

第六章

（一） 翻译练习：将下列句子和词语翻译为英文

1. A wise man will not make himself into a mere machine fit only to do one kind of work.

2. （1） Have no friends not equal to yourself.

（2） Have no friends who are not as yourself.

（3） Befriend his equals.

3. The natural qualities and the results of education are properly blended.

4. A wise and good man sometimes also meets with distress; but a fool when in distress, becomes reckless.

5. A wise and good man hates to die without having done anything to distinguish himself.

6. A scholar, whose mind is set on truth, and who is ashamed of bad clothes and bad food, is not fit to be discoursed with.

7. A wise man who is not serious will not inspire respect; what he learns will not remain permanent.

8. A wise and good man should be distressed that he has no ability; he should never be distressed that men do not take notice of him.

（二） 思考与讨论

略

第七章

（一）翻译练习：将下列句子和词组翻译为英文

1. （1） When we see men of worth, we should think of equaling them.

（2） When we meet with men of worth, we should think how we may equal them.

（3） When you see a man better than you, you should try to equal him.

2. （1） I daily examine myself on three points.

（2） I daily examine into my personal conduct on three points.

（3） I ask myself, said Master Zeng, three questions every day.

3. The general of an army may be carried off, but a man of the common people cannot be robbed of his free will.

4. （1） A fool always has an excuse ready when he does wrong.

（2） An uncultured man would certainly gloss his faults.

5. （1） The superior man is satisfied and composed; the mean man is always full of distress.

（2） A wise and good man is composed and happy; a fool is always worried and full of distress.

6. （1） What the superior man seeks, is in himself. What the mean man seeks, is in others.

（2） A wise man seeks for what he wants in himself; a fool seeks for it from others.

（3） An intelligentleman relies on himself while an uncultured man relies on others.

7. （1） The superior man seeks to perfect the admirable qualities of men.

（2） A good and wise man encourages men to develop the good qualities in their nature.

（3） A cultured man will help others in doing good.

8. The superior man has a dignified ease without pride. The mean man has pride without a dignified ease.

9. A superior man aims high, while an ordinary man directs downward.

10. The superior men harmonize without demanding conformity; the base men demand conformity but not harmonize.

（二）思考与讨论

"樊迟请学稼。子曰：'吾不如老农。'请学为圃，曰：'吾不如老圃。'"樊迟问完话后就出去了，这时，孔子对其他人说："小人哉，樊须也！"此处，理雅各将"小人"译成"small man"，含有贬义（small 有"地位卑微、质量低劣"之意），说樊迟是个"卑微、低劣"之人；威利将"小人"与"君子"对举，说樊迟是"no gentleman"，即"非君子"；辜鸿铭说樊迟是"a petty-minded man"，即"思想狭隘的人"；许渊冲说樊迟是"an uncultured man"，即"没教养的人"。以上四个译本在不同程度上有贬损樊迟之意。谢艳明（2019）认为，孔子在说这句话时，樊迟刚刚离开房间，孔子应该不会背着樊迟就在他人面前贬损他，否则孔子不就成了一个背后骂人的"小人"了？谢艳明（2019）认为，孔子的本意是说樊迟是一个普通人（commoner），关注的是老百姓做的农活，格局不大。"君子"和"小人"在《论语》中常常以并举的形式出现，如"君子怀德，小人怀土；君子怀刑，小人怀惠"（"君子怀念道德，小人怀念乡土；君子关心法度，小人关心恩惠"）。谢艳明（2019）认为"君子"和"小人"在这里并举，并不是德行上的对比，因为"怀德"和"怀刑"虽然是"君子"德行规范的要求（时常记挂着道德礼仪，心中所想的只有仁德和善良，行事时担心自己的行为违反国家法律和社会规范），但是"怀土"和"怀惠"并不是道德低下的表现。理雅各和威利在此分别将"君子"译为 the superior man 和 gentlemen，在翻译"小人"时，威利使用了中性词commoners，即孔子所说的"小老百姓"；而理雅各则使用了带有贬义的 the small man，贬损了原文对"老百姓"的德行规约，从而也贬低了"小人"的文化品格（谢艳明，2019）。

参考文献

Jennings. W. （詹宁斯）*The Confucian "Analects"：A Translation with Annotation and Introduction* ［M］. London：George Routledge and Sons，1895.

Ku，H. M. （辜鸿铭）*The Discourse and Sayings of Confucius：A New Special Translation，Illustrated with Quotations from Goethe and Other Writers* ［M］. Shanghai：Kelly and Walsh，1898.

Legge，J. （理雅各）*Confucian Analects：The Great Learning & the Doctrine of the Mean* ［M］. New York：Dover Publications，1971.

Lin，Y. T. （林语堂）*The Wisdom of Confucius* ［M］. New York：The Modern Library，1938.

Waley，A. （威利）*The Analects of Confucius* ［M］. London：G. Allen & Unwin Ltd. ，1938.

郭著章，黄粉保，毛新耕. 文言英译教程 ［M］. 上海：上海外语教育出版社，2008.

黄国文. 典籍翻译：从语内翻译到语际翻译：以《论语》英译为例 ［J］. 中国外语，2012（6）：64 - 71.

姜哲. 学而时习之，不亦说乎：晚清新教传教士的《论语》英译 ［J］. 中国文化研究，2013（1）：43 - 52.

刘殿爵，杨伯峻. 论语：中英对照版 ［M］. 北京：中华书局，2008.

钱穆. 论语新解 ［M］. 北京：九州出版集团，2011.

天宜.《论语》明心 ［M］. 南京：东南大学出版社，2010.

吴国向. 经典翻译与文化传承："首届《论语》翻译研讨会"简述 ［J］. 中国外语，2012（1）：104 - 107.

吴国向.《论语》翻译版本的语法复杂性研究 ［D］. 广州：中山大学，2013.

谢艳明. 从《论崇高》视角看《论语》英译的文化品格 ［J］. 外国语文研究，2019（1）：63 - 72.

许渊冲. *Confucius Modernized，thus Spoke the Master* ［M］. 北京：高等教育出版社，2005.

杨伯峻. 论语译注［M］. 北京：中华书局，2006.

杨玉英.《论语》分主题读本［M］. 北京：中华书局，2013.

朱熹. 论语集注［M］. 北京：中华书局，1983.

附录 《论语》（1—10篇）英译文（理雅各译）

Book I. HSIO R.

CHAPTER I. 1. The Master said, 'Is it not pleasant to learn with a constant perseverance and application?

2. 'Is it not delightful to have friends coming from distant quarters?

3. 'Is he not a man of complete virtue, who feels no discomposure though men may take no note of him?'

CHAP. II. 1. The philosopher Yû said, 'They are few who, being filial and fraternal, are fond of offending against their superiors. There have been none, who, not liking to offend against their superiors, have been fond of stirring up confusion.

2. 'The superior man bends his attention to what is radical. That being established, all practical courses naturally grow up. Filial piety and fraternal submission! —are they not the root of all benevolent actions?'

CHAP. III. The Master said, 'Fine words and an insinuating appearance are seldom associated with true virtue.'

CHAP. IV. The philosopher Tsăng said, 'I daily examine myself on three points: — whether, in transacting business for others, I may have been not faithful; —whether, in intercourse with friends, I may have been not sincere; —whether I may have not mastered and practised the instructions of my teacher.'

CHAP. V. The Master said, 'To rule a country of a thousand chariots, there must be reverent attention to business, and sincerity; economy in expenditure, and love for men; and the employment of the people at the proper seasons.'

CHAP. VI. The Master said, 'A youth, when at home, should be filial, and, abroad, respectful to his elders. He should be earnest and truthful. He should overflow in love to all, and cultivate the friendship of the good. When he has time and opportunity, after the performance of these things, he should employ them in polite studies.'

CHAP. VII. Tsze-hsiâ said, 'If a man withdraws his mind from the love of beauty, and applies it as sincerely to the love of the virtuous; if, in serving his parents, he can exert his utmost strength; if, in serving his prince, he can devote his life; if in his intercourse with his friends, his words are sincere: —although men say that he has not learned, I will certainly say that he has. '

CHAP. Ⅷ. 1. The Master said, 'If the scholar be not grave, he will not call forth any veneration, and his learning will not be solid.

2. 'Hold faithfulness and sincerity as first principles.

3. 'Have no friends not equal to yourself.

4. 'When you have fault, do not fear to abandon them. '

CHAP. Ⅸ. The philosopher Tsǎng said, 'Let there be a careful attention to perform the funeral rites to parents, and let them be followed when long gone with the ceremonies of sacrifice; —then the virtue of the people will resume its proper excellence. '

CHAP. Ⅹ. 1. Tsze-ch'in asked Tsze-kung, saying, 'When our master comes to any country, he does not fail to learn all about its government. Does he ask his information? or is it given to him?'

2. Tsze-kung said, 'Our Master is benign, upright, courteous, temperate, and complaisant, and thus he gets his information. The Master's mode of asking information! —is it not different from that of other men?'

CHAP. Ⅺ. The Master said, 'While a man's father is alive, look at the bent of his will; when his father is dead, look at his conduct. If for three years he does not alter from the way of his father, he may be called filial. '

CHAP. Ⅻ. 1. The philosopher Yû said, 'In practising the rules of propriety, a natural ease is to be prized. In the ways prescribed by the ancient kings, this is the excellent quality, and in things small and great we follow them.

2. 'Yet it is not to be observed in all cases. If one, knowing how such ease should be prized, manifests it, without regulating it by the rules of propriety, this likewise is not to be done. '

CHAP. ⅩⅢ. The philosopher Yû said, 'When agreements are made according to what is right, what is spoken can be made good. When respect is shown according to what is proper, one keeps far from shame and disgrace. When the parties upon whom a man leans are proper persons to be intimate with, he can make them his guides and masters. '

CHAP. ⅩⅣ. The Master said, 'He who aims to be a man of complete virtue, in his food does not seek to gratify his appetite, nor in his dwelling-place does he seek the appliances of ease; he is earnest in what he is doing, and careful in his speech; he frequents the company of men of-principle that he may be rectified: —such a person may be said indeed to love to learn. '

CHAP. ⅩⅤ. 1. Tsze-kung said, 'What do you pronounce concerning the poor man who yet does not flatter, and the rich man who is not proud?' The Master replied, 'They will do; but they are not equal to him, who, though poor, is yet cheerful, and to him, who, though rich, loves the rules of propriety. '

2. Tsze-kung replied, 'It is said in the *Book of Poetry*, "As you cut and then file, as you carve and then polish. " —The meaning is the same, I apprehend, as that which you have just expressed. '

3. The Master said, 'With one like Ts'ze, I can begin to talk about the *Odes*. I told him one point, and he knew its proper sequence. '

CHAP. XVI. The Master said, 'I will not be afflicted at men's not knowing me; I will be afflicted that I do not know men. '

BOOK II   WEI CHĂNG.

CHAPTER I . The Master said, 'He who exercises government by means of his virtue, may be compared to the north polar star, which keeps its place and all the stars turn towards it. '

CHAP. II . The Master said, 'In the *Book of Poetry* are three hundred pieces, but the design of them all may be embraced in one sentence— "Having no depraved thoughts. " '

CHAP. III. 1. The Master said, 'If the people be led by laws, and uniformity sought to be given them by punishments, they will try to avoid *the punishment*, but have no sense of shame.

2. 'If they be led by virtue, and uniformity sought to be given them by the rules of propriety, they will have the sense of shame, and moreover will become good. '

CHAP. IV. 1. The Master said, 'At fifteen, I had my mind bent on learning.

2. 'At thirty, I stood firm.

3. 'At forty, I had no doubts.

4. 'At fifty, I knew the decrees of heaven.

5. 'At sixty, my ear was an obedient organ *for the reception of truth*.

6. 'At seventy, I could follow what my heart desired, without transgressing what was right. '

CHAP. V. 1. Măng Î asked what filial piety was. The Master said, 'It is not being disobedient. '

2. Soon after, as Fan Ch'ih was driving him, the Master told him, saying, 'Măng-sun asked me what filial piety was, and I answered him, — "not being disobedient. " '

3. Fan Ch'ih said, 'What did you mean?' The Master replied, 'That parents, when alive, should be served according to propriety; that, when dead, they should be buried according to propriety; and that they should be sacrificed to according to

propriety. '

CHAP. Ⅵ. Mǎng Wû asked what filial piety was. The Master said, 'Parents are anxious lest their children should be sick. '

CHAP. Ⅶ. Tsze-yû asked what filial piety was. The Master said, 'The filial piety of nowadays means the support of one's parents. But dogs and horses likewise are able to do something in the way of support; —without reverence, what is there to distinguish the one support given from the other?'

CHAP. Ⅷ. Tsze-hsiâ asked what filial piety was. The Master said, 'The difficulty is with the countenance. If, when their elders have any troublesome affairs, the young take the toil of them, and if when the young have wine and food, they set them before their elders, is THIS to be considered filial piety?'

CHAP. Ⅸ. The Master said, 'I have talked with Hûi for a whole day, and he has not made any objection to any thing I said—as if he were stupid. He has retired, and I have examined his conduct when away from me, and found him able to illustrate my teachings. Hûi ! —He is not stupid. '

CHAP. Ⅹ. 1. The Master said, 'See what a man does.

2. 'Mark his motives.

3. 'Examine in what things he rests.

4. 'How can a man conceal his character!

5. 'How can a man conceal his character!'

CHAP. Ⅺ. The Master said, 'If a man keeps cherishing his old knowledge, so as continually to be acquiring new, he may be a teacher of others. '

CHAP. Ⅻ. The Master said, 'The accomplished scholar is not an utensil. '

CHAP. ⅩⅢ. Tsze-kung asked what constituted the superior man. The Master said, 'He acts before he speaks, and afterwards speaks according to his actions. '

CHAP. ⅩⅣ. The Master said, 'The superior man is catholic and no partizan. The mean man is a partizan and not catholic. '

CHAP. ⅩⅤ. The Master said, 'Learning without thought is labour lost; thought without learning is perilous. '

CHAP. ⅩⅥ. The Master said, 'The study of strange doctrines is injurious indeed!'

CHAP. ⅩⅦ. The Master said, 'Yû, shall I teach you what knowledge is? When you know a thing, to hold that you know it; and when you do not know a thing, to allow that you do not know it; —this is knowledge. '

CHAP. ⅩⅧ. 1. Tsze-chang was learning with a view to official emolument.

2. The Master said, 'Hear much and put aside the points of which you stand in doubt, while you speak cautiously at the same time of the others: —then you will afford

few occasions for blame. See much and put aside the things which seem perilous, while you are cautious at the same time in carrying the others into practice; —then you will have few occasions for repentance. When one gives few occasions for blame in his words, and few occasions for repentance in his conduct, he is in the way to get emolument. '

CHAP. XIX. The duke Ai asked, saying, 'What should be done in order to secure the submission of the people?' Confucius replied, 'Advance the upright and set aside the crooked, then the people will submit. Advance the crooked and set aside the upright, then the people will not submit. '

CHAP. XX. Chî K'ang asked how to cause the people to reverence their ruler, to be faithful to him, and to urge themselves to virtue. The Master said, 'Let him preside over them with gravity; —then they will reverence him. Let him be filial and kind to all; —then they will be faithful to him. Let him advance the good and teach the incompetent; —then they will eagerly seek to be virtuous. '

CHAP. XXI. 1. Some one addressed Confucius, saying, 'Sir, why are you not engaged in the government?'

2. The Master said, 'What does the Shû-king say of filial piety? — "You are filial, you discharge your brotherly duties. These qualities are displayed in government. " This then also constitutes the exercise of government. Why must there be that—making one be in the government. '

CHAP. XXII. The Master said, 'I do not know how a man without truthfulness is to get on. How can a large carriage be made to go without the cross bar for yoking the oxen to, or a small carriage without the arrangement for yoking the horses?'

CHAP. XXIII. 1. Tsze-chang asked whether the affairs of ten ages after could be known.

2. Confucius said, 'The Yin dynasty followed the regulations of the Hsiâ: wherein it took from or added to them may be known. The Châu dynasty has followed the regulations of the Yin: wherein it took from or added to them may be known. Some other may follow the Châu, but though it should be at the distance of a hundred ages, its affairs may be known. '

CHAP. XXIV. 1. The Master said, 'For a man to sacrifice to a spirit which does not belong to him is flattery.

2. 'To see what is right and not to do it is want of courage. '

BOOK III PÂ YIH

CHAPTER I. Confucius said of the head of the Chî family, who had eight rows of pantomimes in his area, 'If he can bear to do this, what may he not bear to do?'

CHAP. II. The three families used the Yung ode, while the vessels were being removed, at the conclusion of the sacrifice. The Master said, ' " Assisting are the princes; —the emperor looks profound and grave. " —what application can these words have in the hail of the three families?'

CHAP. Ⅲ. The Master said, 'If a man be without the virtues proper to humanity, what has he to do with the rites of propriety? If a man be without the virtues proper to humanity, what has he to do with music?'

CHAP. Ⅳ. 1. Lin Fang asked what was the first thing to be attended to in ceremonies.

2. The Master said, 'A great question indeed!'

3. ' In *festive* ceremonies, it is better to be sparing than extravagant. In the ceremonies of mourning, it is better that there be deep sorrow than a minute attention to observances. '

CHAP. Ⅴ. The Master said, 'The rude tribes of the east and north have their princes, and are not like the States of our great land which are without them. '

CHAP. Ⅵ. The chief of the Chî family was about to sacrifice to the Tâi mountain. The Master said to Zan Yû, 'Can you not save him from this?' He answered, 'I cannot. ' Confucius said, 'Alas! Will you say that the Tâi mountain is not so discerning as Lin Fang ?'

CHAP. Ⅶ. The Master said, 'The student of virtue has no contentions. If it be said he cannot avoid them, shall this be in archery? But he bows complaisantly to his competitors; thus he ascends the hall, descends, and exacts the forfeit of drinking. In his contention, he is still the Chün-tsze. '

CHAP. Ⅷ. 1. Tsze-hsiâ asked, saying, 'What is the meaning of the passage—The pretty dimples of her artful smile! The well defined black and white of her eye! The plain ground for the colours?" '

2. The Master said, 'The business of laying on the colours follows the preparation of the plain ground. '

3. 'Ceremonies then are a subsequent thing. ' The Master said, 'It is Shang who can bring out my meaning! Now I can begin to talk about the odes with him. '

CHAP. Ⅸ. The Master said, 'I could describe the ceremonies of the Hsiâ dynasty, but Chî cannot sufficiently attest my words. I am able to describe the ceremonies of the Yin dynasty but Sung cannot sufficiently attest my words. They cannot do so because of the insufficiency of their records and wise men. If those were sufficient, I could adduce them in support of my words. '

CHAP. Ⅹ. The Master said, 'At the great sacrifice, after the pouring out of the libation, I have no wish to look on. '

CHAP. XI. Some one asked the meaning of the great sacrifice. The Master said, 'I do not know. Be who knew its meaning would find it as easy to govern the empire as to look on this;' —pointing to his palm.

CHAP. XII. 1. He sacrificed to the dead, as if they were present. He sacrificed to the spirits, as if the spirits were present.

2. The Master said, 'I consider my not being present at the sacrifice, as if I did not sacrifice. '

CHAP. XIII. 1. Wang-sun Chiâ asked, saying, 'What is the meaning of the saying, "It is better to pay court to the furnace than to the south-west corner?"'

2. The Master said, 'Not so. He who offends against Heaven has none to whom he can pray. '

CHAP. XIV. The Master said, 'Châu had the advantage of viewing the two past dynasties. How complete and elegant are its regulations! I follow Châu. '

CHAP. XV. The Master, when he entered the grand temple, asked about every thing. Some one said, 'Who will say that the son of the man of Tsâu knows the rules of propriety. He has entered the grand temple and asks about every thing. ' The Master heard the remark, and said, 'This is a rule of propriety. '

CHAP. XVI. The Master said, 'In archery it is not *going through* the leather which is the principal thing; —because people's strength is not equal. This was the old way. '

CHAP. XVII. 1. Tsze-kung wished to do away with the offering of a sheep connected with the inauguration of the first day of each month.

2. The Master said, 'Tsze, you love the sheep; I love the ceremony. '

CHAP. XVIII. The Master said, 'The full observance of the rules of propriety in serving one's prince is accounted by people to be flattery. '

CHAP. XIX. The duke Ting asked how a prince should employ his ministers, and how ministers should serve their prince. Confucius replied, 'A prince should employ his ministers according to the rules of propriety; ministers should serve their prince with faithfulness. '

CHAP. XX. The Master said, 'The Kwan Tsü is expressive of enjoyment without being licentious, and of grief without being hurtfully excessive. '

CHAP. XXI. 1. The duke Ai asked Tsâi Wo about the altars of the spirits of the land. Tsâi Wo replied, 'The Hsiâ sovereign used the pine tree; the man of the Yin used the cypress; and the man of the Châu used the chestnut tree, meaning thereby to cause the people to be in awe. '

2. When the Master heard it, he said, 'Things that are done, it is needless to speak about; things that have had their course, it is needless to remonstrate about; things that

are past it is needless to blame. '

CHAP. XXII. 1. The Master said, 'Small indeed was the Capacity of Kwan Chung!'

2. Some one said, 'Was Kwan Chung parsimonious?' 'Kwan,' was the reply, 'had the *San Kwei* and his officers performed no double duties; how can he be considered parsimonious?'

3. 'Then, did Kwan Chung know the rules of propriety?' The Master said, 'The princes of states have a screen intercepting the view at their gates. Kwan had likewise a screen at his gate. The princes of states on any friendly meeting between two of them, had a stand on which to place their inverted cups. Kwan had also such a stand. If Kwan knew the rules of propriety, who does not know them?'

CHAP. XXIII. The Master instructing the Grand music-master of Lü said, 'How to play music may be known. At the commencement of the piece, all the parts should sound together. As it proceeds, they should be in harmony, severally distinct and flowing without break, and thus on to the conclusion. '

CHAP. XXIV. The border-warden at Î requested to be introduced to the Master, saying, 'When men of superior virtue have come to this, I have never been denied the privilege of seeing them. ' The followers of the sage introduced him, and when he came out from the interview, he said, 'My friends, why are you distressed by your master's loss of office? The empire has long been without the principles of truth and right; Heaven is going to use your master as a bell with its wooden tongue. '

CHAP. XXV. The Master said of the Shâo that it was perfectly beautiful and also perfectly good. He said of the Wû that it was perfectly beautiful but not perfectly good.

CHAP. XXVI. The Master said, 'High station filled without indulgent generosity; ceremonies performed without reverence; mourning conducted without sorrow; — wherewith should I contemplate such ways?'

BOOK IV. LE JIN.

CHAPTER I. The Master said, 'It is virtuous manners which constitute the excellence of a neighbourhood. If a man in selecting a residence, do not fix on one where such prevail, how can he be wise?'

CHAP. II. The Master said, 'Those who are without virtue, cannot abide long either in a condition of poverty and hardship, or in a condition of enjoyment. The virtuous rest in virtue; the wise desire virtue. '

CHAP. III. The Master said, 'It is only the truly virtuous man, who can love, or who can hate, others. '

CHAP. IV. The Master said, 'If the will be set on virtue, there will be no practice of wickedness. '

CHAP. V. 1. The Master said, 'Riches and honours are what men desire. If it cannot be obtained in the proper way, they should not be held. Poverty and meanness are what men dislike. If it cannot be obtained in the proper way, they should not be avoided.'

2. 'If a superior man abandon virtue, how can he fulfil the requirements of that name?

3. 'The superior man does not, even for the space of a single meal, act contrary to virtue. In moments of haste, he cleaves to it. In seasons of danger, he cleaves to it.'

CHAP. VI. 1. The Master said, 'I have not seen a person who loved virtue, or one who hated what was not virtuous. He who loved virtue, would esteem nothing above it. He who hated what is not virtuous, would practise virtue in such a way that he would not allow any thing that is not virtuous to approach his person.

2. 'Is any one able for one day to apply his strength to virtue? I have not seen the case in which his strength would be insufficient.

3. 'Should there possibly be any such case, I have not seen it.'

CHAP. VII. The Master said, 'The faults of men are characteristic of the class to which they belong. By observing a man's faults, it may be known that he is virtuous.'

CHAP. VIII. The Master said, 'If a man in the morning hear the right way, he may die in the evening without regret.'

CHAP. IX. The Master said, 'A scholar, whose mind is set on truth, and who is ashamed of bad clothes and bad food, is not fit to be discoursed with.'

CHAP. X. The Master said, 'The superior man, in the world, does not set his mind either for any thing, or against any thing; what is right he will follow.'

CHAP. XI. The Master said, 'The superior man thinks of virtue; the small man thinks of comfort. The superior man thinks of the sanctions of law; the small man thinks of favours which he may receive.'

CHAP. XII. The Master said, 'He who acts with a constant view to his own advantage will be much murmured against.'

CHAP. XIII. The Master said, 'Is a prince able to govern his kingdom with the complaisance proper to the rules of propriety, what difficulty will he have? If he cannot govern it with that complaisance, what has he to do with the rules of propriety?'

CHAP. XIV. The Master said, 'A man should say, I am not concerned that I have no place, I am concerned how I may fit myself for one. I am not concerned that I am not known, I seek to be worthy to be known.'

CHAP. XV. 1. The Master said, 'Shăn, my doctrine is that of an all-pervading unity.' The disciple Tsăng replied, 'Yes.'

2. The Master went out, and the other disciples asked, saying, 'What do his words

mean?' Tsăng said, 'The doctrine of our master is to be true to the principles of our nature and the benevolent exercise of them to others, —this and nothing more.'

CHAP. XVI. The Master said, 'The mind of the superior man is conversant with righteousness; the mind of the mean man is conversant with gain.'

CHAP. XVII. The Master said, 'When we see men of worth, we should think of equaling them; when we see men of a contrary character, we should turn inwards and examine ourselves.'

CHAP. XVIII. The Master said, 'In serving his parents, a son may remonstrate with them, but gently; when he sees that they do not incline to follow his advice, he shows an increased degree of reverence, but does not abandon his purpose; and should they punish him, he does not allow himself to murmur.'

CHAP. XIX. The Master said, 'While his parents are alive, *the son* may not go abroad to a distance. If he does go abroad, he must have a fixed place to which he goes.'

CHAP. XX. The Master said, 'If the son for three years does not alter from the way of his father, he may be called filial.'

CHAP. XXI. The Master said, 'The years of parents may by no means not be kept in the memory, as an occasion at once for joy and for fear.'

CHAP. XXII. The Master said, 'The reason why the ancients did not readily give utterance to their words, was that they feared lest their actions should not come up to them.'

CHAP. XXIII. The Master said, 'The cautious seldom err.'

CHAP. XXIV. The Master said, 'The superior man wishes to be slow in his words and earnest in his conduct.'

CHAP. XXV. The Master said, 'Virtue is not left to stand alone. He who practises it will have neighbors.'

CHAP. XXVI. Tsze-yû said, 'In serving a prince, frequent remonstrances lead to disgrace. Between friends, frequent reproofs make the friendship distant.'

BOOK V. KUNG-YÊ CH'ANG.

CHAPTER I. 1. The Master said of Kung-yê Ch'ang that he might be wived; although he was put in bonds, he had not been guilty of any crime. Accordingly, he gave him his own daughter to wife.

2. Of Nan Yung he said that if the country were well governed, he would not be out of office, and if it were ill governed, he would escape punishment and disgrace. He gave him the daughter of his own elder brother to wife.

CHAP. II. The Master said of Tsze-chien, 'Of superior virtue indeed is such a man! If there were not virtuous men in Lû, how could this man have acquired this character?'

CHAP. Ⅲ. Tsze-kung asked, 'What do you say of me, Ts'ze?' The Master said, 'You are an utensil.' 'What utensil?' 'A gemmed sacrificial utensil.'

CHAP. Ⅳ. 1. Some one said, 'Yung is truly virtuous, but he is not ready with his tongue.'

2. The Master said, 'What is the good of being ready with the tongue? They who meet men with smartnesses of speech, for the most part procure themselves hatred. I know not whether he be truly virtuous, but why should he show readiness of the tongue?'

CHAP. Ⅴ. The Master was wishing Ch'i-tiâo K'âi to enter on official employment. He replied, 'I am not yet able to rest in the assurance of THIS.' The Master was pleased.

CHAP. Ⅵ. The Master said, 'My doctrines make no way. I will get upon a raft and float about on the sea. He that will accompany me will be Yû, I dare to say.' Tsze-lû hearing this was glad, upon which the Master said, 'Yû is fonder of daring than I am. He does not exercise his judgment upon matters.'

CHAP. Ⅶ. 1. Măng Wû asked about Tsze-lû, whether he was perfectly virtuous. The Master said, 'I do not know.'

2. He asked again, when the Master replied, 'In a kingdom of a thousand chariots, Yû might be employed to manage the military levies, but I do not know whether he be perfectly virtuous.'

3. 'And what do you say of Ch'iû?' The Master replied, 'In a city of a thousand families, or a house of a hundred chariots, Ch'ih might be employed as governor, but I do not know whether he is perfectly virtuous.'

4. 'What do you say of Ch'ih?' The Master replied, 'With his sash girt and standing in a court, Ch'ih might be employed to converse with the visitors and guests, but I do not know whether he is perfectly virtuous.'

CHAP. Ⅷ. 1. The Master said to Tsze-kung, 'Which do you consider superior, yourself or Hui?'

2. Tsze-kung replied, 'How dare I compare myself with Hûi? Hûi hears one point and knows all about a subject; I hear one point and know a second.'

3. The Master said, 'You are not equal to him. I grant you, you are not equal to him.'

CHAP. Ⅸ. 1. Tsâi Yu being asleep during the day time, the Master said, 'Rotten wood cannot be carved; a wall of dirty earth will not receive the trowel. This Yü! —what is the use of my reproving him?'

2. The Master said, 'At first, my way with men was to hear their words, and give them credit for their conduct. Now my way is to hear their words, and look at their conduct. It is from Yü that I have learned to make this change.'

CHAP. X. The Master said, ' I have not seen a firm and unbending man. ' Some one replied, ' There is Shǎn Ch'ang. ' ' Ch'ang. 'said the Master, ' is under the influence of his passions; how can he be pronounced firm and unbending?'

CHAP. XI. Tsze-kung said, ' What I do not wish men to do to me, I also wish not to do to men. ' The Master said, ' Ts'ze, you have not attained to that. '

CHAP. XII. Tsze-kung said, ' The Master's personal displays of his principles, and ordinary descriptions of them may be heard. His discourses about man's nature, and the way of Heaven, cannot be heard. '

CHAP. XIII. When Tsze-lû heard anything, if he had not yet succeeded in carrying it into practice, he was only afraid lest he should hear something else.

CHAP. XIV. Tsze-kung asked, saying, ' On what ground did Kung-wǎn get that title of wǎn?' The Master said. ' He was of an active nature and yet fond of learning, and he was not ashamed to ask and learn of his inferiors! On these grounds he has been styled WÀN. '

CHAP. XV. The Master said of Tsze-ch'an that he had four of the characteristics of a superior man:—in his conduct of himself, he was humble; in serving his superiors, he was respectful; in nourishing the people, he was kind; in ordering the people, he was just.

CHAP. XVI. The Master said, ' Yen P'ing knew well how to maintain friendly intercourse. The acquaintance might be long, but he showed the *same* respect *as at first.* '

CHAP. XVII. The Master said, ' Tsang Wǎn kept a large tortoise in a house, on the capitals of the pillars of which he had hills made, with representations of duckweed on the small pillars above the beams supporting the rafters. —Of what sort was his wisdom?'

CHAP. XVIII. 1. Tsze-chang asked, saying, ' The minister Tsze-wǎn, thrice took office, and manifested no joy in his countenance. Thrice he retired from office, and manifested no displeasure. He made it a point to inform the new minister of the way in which he had conducted the government; —what do you say of him?' The Master replied, ' He was loyal. ' ' Was he perfectly virtuous?' ' I do not know. How can he be pronounced perfectly virtuous?'

2. Tsze-chang proceeded, ' When the officer Ch'ûi killed the prince of Chi, Ch'an Wǎn, though he was the owner of forty horses, abandoned them and left the country. Coming to another state, he said, "They are here like our great officer, Ch'ûi " and left it. He came to a second state, and with the same observation left it also ; —what do you say of him?' The Master replied, ' He was pure. ' ' Was he perfectly virtuous?' ' I do not know. How can he be pronounced perfectly virtuous?'

CHAP. XIX. Chî Wǎn thought thrice, and then acted. When the Master was informed of it, he said, 'Twice may do. '

CHAP. XX. The Master said, 'When good order prevailed in his country, Ning Wû acted the part of a wise man. When his country was in disorder, he acted the part of a stupid man. Others may equal his wisdom, but they cannot equal his stupidity. '

CHAP. XXI. When the Master was in Ch'ân, he said, 'Let me return! Let me return! The little children of my school are ambitious and too hasty. They are accomplished and complete so far, but they do not know how to restrict and shape themselves. '

CHAP. XXII. The Master said, 'Po-î and Shû-ch'î did not keep the former wickednesses of men in mind, and hence the resentments directed towards them were few. '

CHAP. XXIII. The Master said, 'Who says of Wei-shang Kâo that he is upright? One begged some vinegar of him, and he begged it of a neighbour and gave it to the man. '

CHAP. XXIV. The Master said, 'Fine words, an insinuating appearance, and excessive respect; —Tso Ch'iû-ming was ashamed of them. I also am ashamed of them. To conceal resentment against a person, and appear friendly with him; —Tso Ch'iû-ming was ashamed of such conduct. I also am ashamed of it. '

CHAP. XXV. 1. Yen Yüan and Chî Lû being by his side, the Master said to them, 'Come, let each of you tell his wishes. '

2. Tsze-lû said, 'I should like, having chariots and horses, and light fur dresses, to share them with my friends, and though they should spoil them, I would not be displeased. '

3. Yen Yüan said, 'I should like not to boast of my excellence, nor to make a display of my meritorious deeds. '

4. Tsze-lû then said, 'I should like, sir, to hear your wishes. ' The Master said, 'They are, in regard to the aged, to give them rest; in regard to friends, to show them sincerity; in regard to the young, to treat them tenderly. '

CHAP. XXVI. The Master said, 'It is all over! I have not yet seen one who could perceive his faults, and inwardly accuse himself. '

CHAP. XXVII. The Master said, 'In a hamlet of ten families, there may be found one honourable and sincere as I am, but not so fond of learning. '

BOOK VI YUNG YÊY.

CHAPTER. I. 1. The Master said, 'There is Yung! —He might occupy the place of a prince. '

2. Chung-kung asked about Tsze-sang Po-tsze. The Master said, 'He may pass. He does not mind small matters. '

3. Chung-kung said, 'If a man *cherish* in himself a reverential feeling of the necessity

of attention to business, though he may be easy in small matters in his government of the people, that may be allowed. But if he cherish in himself that easy feeling, and also carry it out in his practice, is not such an easy mode of procedure excessive?'

4. The Master said, 'Yung's words are right. '

CHAP. II. The duke Âi asked which of the disciples loved to learn. Confucius replied to him, 'There was Yen Hûi; HE loved to learn. He did not transfer his anger; he did not repeat a fault. Unfortunately, his appointed time was short and he died; and now there is not such another. I have not yet heard of any one who loves to learn as he did. '

CHAP. III. 1. Tsze-hwâ being employed on a mission to Ch'î, the disciple Zan requested grain for his mother. The Master said, 'Give her a *fû*. ' *Yen* requested more. 'Give her an *yü*, ' said the Master. Yen gave her five *ping*.

2. The Master said, 'When Ch'ih was proceeding to Ch'î, he had fat horses to his carriage, and wore light furs. I have heard that a superior man helps the distressed, but does not add to the wealth of the rich. '

3. Yüan Sze being made governor of his town by the Master, he gave him nine hundred measures of grain, but Sze declined them.

4. The Master said, 'Do not decline them. May you not give them away in the neighborhoods, hamlets, towns, and villages?'

CHAP. IV. The Master, speaking of Chung-kung, said, 'If the calf of a brindled cow be red and horned, although man may not wish to use it, would the spirits of the mountains and rivers put it aside?'

CHAP. V. The Master said, 'Such was Hûi that for three months there would be nothing in his mind contrary to perfect virtue. The others may attain to this on some days or in some months, but nothing more. '

CHAP. VI. Chi K'ang asked about Chung-yû, whether he was fit to be employed as an officer of government. The Master said, 'Yû is a man of decision; what difficulty would he find in being an officer of government ?' K'ang asked, 'Is Tsǎze fit to be employed as an officer of government?' and was answered, 'Tsǎze is a man of intelligence; what difficulty would he find in being an officer of government?' And to the same question about Ch'iû the Master gave the same reply, saying, 'Ch'iû is a man of various ability. '

CHAP. VII. The chief of the Chî family sent to ask Min Tsze-ch'ien to be governor of Pî. Min Tsze-ch'ien said, 'Decline the offer for me politely. If any one come again to me with a second invitation, I shall be obliged to go and live on the banks of the Wǎn. '

CHAP. VIII. Bo-niû being sick, the Master went to ask for him. He took hold of his hand through the window, and said, 'It is killing him. It is the appointment of Heaven, alas! That such a man should have such a sickness! That such a man should have such a sickness！'

CHAP. Ⅸ. The Master said, 'Admirable indeed was the virtue of Hûi! With a single bamboo dish of rice, a single gourd dish of drink, and living in his mean narrow lane, while others could not have endured the distress, he did not allow his joy to be affected by it. Admirable indeed was the virtue of Hûi！'

CHAP. Ⅹ. Yen Ch'iû said, 'It is not that I do not delight in your doctrines, but my strength is insufficient.' The Master said, 'Those whose strength is insufficient give over in the middle of the way, but now you limit yourself.'

CHAP. Ⅺ. The Master said to Tsze-hsià, 'Do you be a scholar after the style of the superior man, and not after that of the mean man.'

CHAP. Ⅻ. Tsze-yû being governor of Wû-ch'ng, the Master said to him, 'Have you got good men there？' He answered, 'There is Tan-t'âi Mie-ming, who never in walking takes a short cut, and never comes to my office, excepting on public business.'

CHAP. ⅩⅢ. The Master said, 'Măng Chih-fan does not boast of his merit. Being in the rear on an occasion of flight, when they were about to enter the gate, he whipped up his horse saying, "It is not that I dare to be last. My horse would not advance."'

CHAP. ⅩⅣ. The Master said, 'Without the specious speech of the litanist T'o and the beauty of *the prince* Châo of Sung, it is difficult to escape in the present age.'

CHAP. ⅩⅤ. The Master said, 'Who can go out but by the door？ How is it that men will not walk according to these ways？'

CHAP. ⅩⅥ. The Master said, 'Where the solid qualities are in excess of accomplishments, we have rusticity; where the accomplishments are in excess of the solid qualities, we have the manners of a clerk. When the accomplishments and solid qualities are equally blended, we then have the man of complete virtue.'

CHAP. ⅩⅦ. The Master said, 'Man is born for uprightness. If a man lose his uprightness, and yet live, his escape from death is the effect of mere good fortune.'

CHAP. ⅩⅧ. The Master said, 'They who know the truth are not equal to those who love it, and they who love it are not equal to those who find pleasure in it.'

CHAP. ⅩⅨ. The Master said, 'To those whose talents are above mediocrity, the highest subjects may be announced. To those who are below mediocrity, the highest subjects may not be announced.'

CHAP. ⅩⅩ. Fan Ch'ih asked what constituted wisdom. The Master said, 'To give one's self earnestly to the duties due to men, and, while respecting spiritual beings, to keep aloof from them, may be called wisdom.' He asked about perfect virtue. The Master said, 'The man of virtue makes the difficulty to be overcome his first business, and success only a subsequent consideration; —this may be called perfect virtue.'

CHAP. XXI. The Master said, 'The wise find pleasure in water; the virtuous find pleasure in hills. The wise are active; the virtuous are tranquil. The wise are joyful, the virtuous are long-lived. '

CHAP. XXII. The Master said, 'Ch'i, by one change, would come to the state of Lû. Lû, by one change, would come to a state where true principles predominated. '

CHAP. XXIII. The Master said, 'A cornered vessel without corners. A strange cornered vessel! A strange cornered vessel!'

CHAP. XXIV. Tsâi Wo asked, saying, 'A benevolent man, though it be told him, — "There is a man in the well" will go in after him, I suppose. ' Confucius said, 'Why should he do so? A superior man may be made to go to the well, but he cannot be made to go down into it. He may be imposed upon, but he cannot be fooled. '

CHAP. XXV. The Master said, 'The superior man, extensively studying all learning, and keeping himself under the restraint of the rules of propriety, may thus likewise not overstep what is right. '

CHAP. XXVI. The Master having visited Nan-tsze, Tsze-lû was displeased, on which the Master swore, saying, 'Wherein I have done improperly, may Heaven reject me! may Heaven reject me!'

CHAP. XXVII. The Master said, 'Perfect is the virtue which is according to the Constant Mean! Rare for a long time has been its practice among the people. '

CHAP. XXVIII. 1. Tsze-kung said, 'Suppose the case of a man extensively conferring benefits on the people, and able to assist all, what would you say of him? Might he be called perfectly virtuous?' The Master said, 'Why speak only of virtue in connection with him! Must he not have the qualities of a sage? Even Yâo and Shun were still solicitous about this.

2. 'Now the man of perfect virtue, wishing to be established himself, seeks also to establish others; wishing to be enlarged himself, he seeks also to enlarge others.

3. 'To be able to judge of others by what is nigh *in ourselves*; —this may be called the art of virtue. '

BOOK VII SHûR

CHAPTER I. The Master said, 'A transmitter and not a maker, believing in and loving the ancients, I venture to compare myself with our old P'ǎng. '

CHAP. II. The Master said, 'The silent treasuring up of knowledge; learning without satiety; and instructing others without being wearied: — what one of these things belongs to me?'

CHAP. III. The Master said, 'The leaving virtue without proper cultivation; the not thoroughly discussing what is learned; not being able to move towards righteousness of which a knowledge is gained; and not being able to change what is not good: — these are the things which occasion me solicitude.'

CHAP. Ⅳ. When the Master was unoccupied with business, his manner was easy, and he looked pleased.

CHAP. Ⅴ. The Master said, 'Extreme is my decay. For a long time, I have not dreamed, as I was wont to do, that I saw the duke of Châu.'

CHAP. Ⅵ. 1. The Master said, 'Let the will be set on the path of duty.

2. 'Let every attainment in what is good be firmly grasped.

3. 'Let perfect virtue be accorded with.

4. 'Let relaxation and enjoyment be found in the polite arts.'

CHAP. Ⅶ. The Master said, 'From the man bringing his bundle of dried flesh for my teaching upwards, I have never refused instruction to any one.'

CHAP. Ⅷ. The Master said, 'I do not open up the truth to one who is not eager to get knowledge, nor help out any one who is not anxious to explain himself. When I have presented one corner of a subject to any one, and he cannot from it learn the other three, I do not repeat my lesson.'

CHAP. Ⅸ. 1. When the Master was eating by the side of a mourner, he never ate to the full.

2. He did not sing on the same day in which he had been weeping.

CHAP. Ⅹ. 1. The Master said to Yen Yüan, 'When called to office to undertake its duties; when not so called, to lie retired; —it is only I and you who have attained to this.'

2. Tsze-lû said, 'If you had the conduct of the armies of a great state, whom would you have to act with you?'

3. The Master said, 'I would not have him to act with me, who will unarmed attack a tiger, or cross a river without a boat, dying without any regret. My associate must be the man who proceeds to action full of solicitude, who is fond of adjusting his plans, and then carries them into execution.'

CHAP. Ⅺ. The Master said, 'If the search for riches is sure to be successful, though I should become a groom with whip in hand to get them, I will do so. As the search may not be successful, I will follow after that which I love.'

CHAP. Ⅻ. The things in reference to which the Master exercised the greatest caution were—fasting, war, and sickness.

CHAP. ⅩⅢ. When the Master was in Ch'î, he heard the Shâo, and for three months did not know the taste of flesh. 'I did not think,' he said, 'that music could have been made so excellent as this.'

CHAP. XIV. 1. Yen Yû said, 'Is our Master for the prince of Wei?' Tsze-kung said, 'Oh! I will ask him'

2. He went in accordingly, and said, 'What sort of men were Po-î and Shû-ch'î ?' 'They were ancient worthies, 'said the Master. ' Did they have any repinings because of their course?' The Master again replied, 'They sought to act virtuously, and they did so; and what was there for them to repine about?' On this, Tsze-kung went out and said, 'Our Master is not for him. '

CHAP. XV. The Master said, 'With coarse rice to eat, with water to drink, and my bended arm for a pillow; —I have still joy in the midst of these things. Riches and honours acquired by unrighteousness are to me as a floating cloud. '

CHAP. XVI. The Master said, 'If some years were added to my life, I would give fifty to the study of the Yî, and then I might come to be without great faults. '

CHAP. XVII. The Master's frequent themes of discourse were—the *Odes*, the History, and the maintenance of the Rules of Propriety. On all these he frequently discoursed.

CHAP. XVIII. 1. The duke of Sheh asked Tsze-lû about Confucius, and Tsze-lû did not answer him.

2. The Master said, 'Why did you not say to him, —He is simply a man, who in his eager pursuit of knowledge forgets his food, who in the joy of its attainment forgets his sorrows, and who does not perceive that old age is coming on?'

CHAP. XIX. The Master said, 'I am not one who was born in the possession of knowledge; I am one who is fond of antiquity, and earnest in seeking it there. '

CHAP. XX. The subjects on which the Master did not talk, were— extraordinary things, feats of strength, disorder, and spiritual beings.

CHAP. XXI. The Master said, 'When I walk along with two others, they may serve me as my teachers. I will select their good qualities and follow them, their bad qualities and avoid them. '

CHAP. XXII. The Master said, 'Heaven produced the virtue that is in me. Hwan T'ûi — what can he do to me?'

CHAP. X X III. The Master said, 'Do you think, my disciple that I have any concealments? I conceal nothing from you. There is nothing which I do that is not shown to you, my disciples; —that is my way. '

CHAP. XXIV. There were four things which the Master taught, —letters, ethics, devotion of soul, and truthfulness.

CHAP. XXV. 1. The Master said, 'A sage it is not mine to see; could I see a man of real talent and virtue, that would satisfy me. '

2. The Master said, 'A good man it is not mine to see; could I see a man possessed

of constancy, that would satisfy me.

3. 'Having not and yet affecting to have, empty and yet affecting to be full, straightened and yet affecting to be at ease; —it is difficult with such characteristics to have constancy. '

CHAP. XXVI. The Master angled, —but did not use a net. He shot, —but not at birds perching.

CHAP. XXVII. The Master said, 'There may be those who act without knowing why. I do not do so. Hearing much and selecting what is good and following it, seeing much and keeping it in memory; this is the second style of knowledge. '

CHAP. XXVIII. 1. It was difficult to talk (profitably and reputably) with the people of Hû-hsiang, and a lad of that place having had an interview with the Master, the disciples doubted.

2. The Master said, 'I admit people's approach to me without committing myself as to what they may do when they have retired. Why must one be so severe? If a man purify himself to wait upon me, I receive him so purified, without guaranteeing his past conduct. '

CHAP. XXIX. The Master said, 'Is virtue a thing remote? I wish to be virtuous, and lo! Virtue is at hand. '

CHAP. XXX. 1. The minister of crime of Ch'ǎn asked whether the duke Châo knew propriety, and Confucius said, 'He knew propriety. '

2. Confucius having retired, the minister bowed to Wû-mâ Ch'î to come forward, and said, 'I have heard that the superior man is not a partizan. May the superior man be a partizan also? The prince married a daughter of the house of Wû, of the same surname with himself; and called her, — "The elder Tsze of Wû. " If the prince knew propriety, who does not know it?'

3. Wû-mâ Ch'î reported these remarks, and the Master said, 'I am fortunate! If I have any errors, people are sure to know them. '

CHAP. XXXI. When the Master was in company with a person who was singing, if he sang well, he would make him repeat the song, while he accompanied it with his own voice.

CHAP. XXXII. The Master said, 'In letters I am perhaps equal to other men, but the character of the superior man, carrying out in his conduct what he professes, is what I have not yet attained to. '

CHAP. XXXIII. The Master said, 'The sage and the man of perfect virtue; —how dare I rank myself with them? It may simply be said of me, that I strive to become such without satiety, and teach others without weariness. ' Kung-hsî Hwâ said, 'This is just what we, the disciples, cannot imitate you in. '

CHAP. XXXIV. The Master being very sick, Tsze-lû asked leave to pray for him. He said, 'May such a thing be done ?' Tsze-lû replied, 'It may. In the Eulogies it is said, "Prayer has been made for thee to the spirits of the upper and lower worlds. "' The Master said, 'My praying has been for a long time. '

CHAP. XXXV. The Master said, 'Extravagance leads to insubordination, and parsimony to meanness. It is better to be mean than to be insubordinate. '

CHAP. XXXVI. The Master said, 'The superior man is satisfied and composed; the mean man is always full of distress. '

CHAP. XXXVII. The Master was mild, and yet dignified; majestic, and yet not fierce; respectful, and yet easy.

BOOK VIII   T'ÂI-Po

CHAPTER I. The Master said, 'T'âi-po may be said to have reached the highest point of virtuous action. Thrice he declined the empire, and the people *in ignorance of his motives* could not express their approbation of his conduct. '

CHAP. II. 1. The Master said, 'Respectfulness, without the rules of propriety, becomes laborious bustle; carefulness, without the rules of propriety, becomes timidity; boldness, without the rules of propriety, becomes insubordination; straightforwardness, without the rules of propriety, becomes rudeness.

2. 'When those who are in high stations perform well all their duties to their relations, the people are aroused to virtue. When old friends are not neglected by them, the people are preserved from meanness. '

CHAP. III. The philosopher Tsăng being sick, he called to him the disciples of his school, and said, 'Uncover my feet, uncover my hands. It is said in the *Book of Poetry*, "We should be apprehensive and cautious, as if on the brink of a deep gulf, as if treading on thin ice. " And so have I been. Now and hereafter, I know my escape from all injury to my person, O ye, my little children. '

CHAP. IV. 1. The philosopher Tsăng being sick, Măng Ch'ăng went to ask how he was.

2. Tsăng said to him, 'When a bird is about to die, its notes are mournful; when a man is about to die, his words are good.

3. 'There are three principles of conduct which the man of high rank should consider specially important: —that in his deportment and manner he keep from violence and heedlessness; that in regulating his countenance he keep near to sincerity; and that in his words and tones he keep far from lowness and impropriety. As to such matters as attending to the sacrificial vessels, there are the proper officers for them. '

CHAP. V. The philosopher Tsăng said, 'Gifted with ability, and yet putting questions to those who were not so; possessed of much, and yet putting questions to those possessed of little; having, as though he had not; full, and yet counting himself as empty; offended against, and yet entering into no altercation: formerly I had a friend who pursued this style of conduct.'

CHAP. VI. The philosopher Tsăng said, 'Suppose that there is an individual who can be entrusted with the charge of a young orphan *prince*, and can be commissioned with authority over a state of a hundred li, and whom no emergency however great can drive from his principles; —is such a man a superior man? He is a superior man indeed.'

CHAP. VII. 1. The philosopher Tsăng said, 'The scholar may not be without breadth of mind and vigorous endurance. His burden is heavy and his course is long.

2. 'Perfect virtue is the burden which he considers it is his to sustain; —is it not heavy? Only with death does his course stop; —is it not long?'

CHAP. VIII. 1. The Master said, 'It is by the *Odes* that the mind is aroused.

2. 'It is by the *Rules* of propriety that the character is established.

3. 'It is from *Music* that the finish is received.'

CHAP. IX. The Master said, 'The people may be made to follow a path of action, but they may not be made to understand it.'

CHAP. X. The Master said, 'The man who is fond of daring and is dissatisfied with poverty, will proceed to insubordination. So will the man who is not virtuous, when you carry your dislike of him to an extreme.'

CHAP. XI. The Master said, 'Though a man have abilities as admirable as those of the duke of Châu, yet if he be proud and niggardly, those other things are really not worth being looked at.'

CHAP. XII. The Master said, 'It is not easy to find a man who has learned for three years without coming to be good.'

CHAP. XIII. 1. The Master said, 'With sincere faith he unites the love of learning; holding firm to death, he is perfecting the excellence of his course.

2. 'Such an one will not enter a tottering state, nor dwell in a disorganized one. When right principles of government prevail in the kingdom, he will show himself; when they are prostrated, he will keep concealed.

3. 'When a country is well governed, poverty and a mean condition are things to be ashamed of: When a country is ill governed, riches and honour are things to be ashamed of.'

CHAP. XIV. The Master said, 'He who is not in any particular office, has nothing to do with plans for the administration of its duties.'

CHAP. ⅩⅤ. The Master said, 'When the music-master Chih first entered on his office, the finish with the Kwan Tsü was magnificent; —how it filled the ears!'

CHAP. ⅩⅥ. The Master said, 'Ardent and yet not upright; stupid and yet not attentive; simple and yet not sincere: —such persons I do not understand.'

CHAP. ⅩⅦ. The Master said, 'Learn as if you could not reach your object, and were always fearing also lest you should lose it.'

CHAP. ⅩⅧ. The Master said, 'How majestic was the manner in which Shun and Yü held possession of the empire, as if it were nothing to them!'

CHAP. ⅪⅩ. 1. The Master said, 'Great indeed was Yâo as a sovereign! How majestic was he! It is only Heaven that is grand, and only Yâo corresponded to it. How vast was his virtue! The people could find no name for it.

2. 'How majestic was he in the works which he accomplished! How glorious in the elegant regulations which he instituted!'

CHAP. ⅩⅩ. 1. Shun had five ministers, and the empire was well governed.

2. King Wû said, 'I have ten able ministers.'

3. Confucius said, 'Is not *the saying* that talents are difficult to find, true? Only when the dynasties of T'ang and Yü met, were they more abundant than in this of Châu, yet there was a woman among them. The able ministers were no more than nine men.

4. 'King Wăn possessed two of the three parts of the empire, and with those he served the dynasty of Yin. The virtue of the house of Châu may be said to have reached the highest point indeed.'

CHAP. ⅩⅪ. The Master said, 'I can find no flaw in the character of Yü. He used himself coarse food and drink, but displayed the utmost filial piety towards the spirits. His ordinary garments were poor but he displayed the utmost elegance in his sacrificial cap and apron. He lived in a low mean house, but expended all his strength on the ditches and water-channels. I can find nothing like a flaw in Yü.'

BOOK Ⅸ. TSZE HAN.

CHAPTER Ⅰ. The subjects of which the Master seldom spoke were— profitableness, and also the appointments of Heaven, and perfect virtue.

CHAP. Ⅱ. 1. A man of the village of Tâ-hsiang said, 'Great indeed is the philosopher K'ung! His learning is extensive, and yet he does not render his name famous by any *particular* thing.'

2. The Master heard the observation, and said to his disciples, 'What shall I practice? Shall I practice charioteering, or shall I practice archery? I will practice charioteering.'

CHAP. Ⅲ. 1. The Master said, 'The linen cap is that prescribed by the rules of ceremony, but now a silk one is worn. It is economical, and I follow the common practice.

2. 'The rules of ceremony prescribe the bowing below the hail, but now the practice is to bow only after ascending it. That is arrogant. I continue to bow below the hail, though I oppose the common practice. '

CHAP. Ⅳ. There were four things from which the Master was entirely free. He had no foregone conclusions, no arbitrary predeterminations, no obstinacy, and no egoism.

CHAP. Ⅴ. 1. The Master was put in fear in K'wang.

2. He said, 'After the death of king Wǎn, was not the cause of truth lodged here in me?

3. 'If Heaven had wished to let this cause of truth perish, then I, a future mortal, should not have got such a relation to that cause. While Heaven does not let the cause of truth perish, what can the people of K'wang do to me ?'

CHAP. Ⅵ. 1. A high officer asked Tsze-kung saying, 'May we not say that your Master is a sage? How various is his ability!'

2. Tsze Kung said, 'Certainly Heaven has endowed him unlimitedly. He is about a sage. And, moreover, his ability is various. '

3. The Master heard the conversation and said, 'Does the high officer know me? When I was young, my condition was low, and therefore I acquired my ability in many things, but they were mean matters. Must the superior man have such variety of ability? He does not need variety of ability. '

4. Lâo said, 'The Master said, "Having no official employment, I acquired many arts. " '

CHAP. Ⅶ. The Master said, 'Am I indeed possessed of knowledge? I am not knowing. But if a mean person, who appears quite empty-like, ask anything of me, I set it forth from one end to the other, and exhaust it. '

CHAP. Ⅷ. The Master said, 'The FǍNG bird does not come; the river sends forth no map: —it is all over with me!'

CHAP. Ⅸ. When the Master saw a person in a mourning dress, or any one with the cap and upper and lower garments of full dress, or a blind person, on observing them approaching, though they were younger than himself, he would rise up, and if he had to pass by them he would do so hastily.

CHAP. Ⅹ. 1. Yen Yüan, in admiration of the Master's doctrines, sighed and said, 'I looked up to them, and they seemed to become more high; I tried to penetrate them, and they seemed to become more firm; I looked at them before me, and suddenly they seemed to be behind.

2. 'The Master, by orderly method, skilfully leads men on. He enlarged my mind with learning, and taught me the restraints of propriety.

3. 'When I wish to give over the study of his doctrines, I cannot do so, and having exerted all my ability, there seems something to stand right up before me; but though I wish to follow and lay hold of it, I really find no way to do so. '

CHAP. XI. 1. The Master being very ill, Tsze-lû wished the disciples to act as ministers to him.

2. During a remission of his illness, he said, 'Long has the conduct of Yû been deceitful! By pretending to have ministers when I have them not, whom should I impose upon? Should I impose upon Heaven?

3. 'Moreover, than that I should die in the hands of ministers, is it not better that I should die in the hands of you, my disciples? And though I may not get a great burial, shall I die upon the road?'

CHAP. XII. Tsze-kung said, 'There is a beautiful gem here. Should I lay it up in a case and keep it? or should I seek for a good price and sell it?' The Master said, 'Sell it! Sell it! But I would wait till the price was offered. '

CHAP. XIII. 1. The Master was wishing to go and live among the nine wild tribes of the east.

2. Some one said, 'They are rude. How can you do such a thing?' The Master said, 'If a superior man dwelt among them, what rudeness would there be?'

CHAP. XIV. The Master said, 'I returned from Wei to Lû, and then the music was reformed, and the pieces in the Imperial songs and Praise songs found all their proper places. '

CHAP. XV. The Master said, 'Abroad, to serve the high ministers and officers; at home, to serve one's father and elder brother; in all duties to the dead, not to dare not to exert one's self; and not to be overcome of wine: —which one of these things do I attain to?'

CHAP. XVI. The Master standing by a stream, said, 'It passes on just like this, not ceasing day or night!'

CHAP. XVII. The Master said, 'I have not seen one who loves virtue as he loves beauty. '

CHAP. XVIII. The Master said, 'The prosecution of learning may be compared to what may happen in raising a mound. If there want but one basket of earth to complete the work, and I stop, the stopping is my own work. It may be compared to throwing down the earth on the level ground. Though but one basketful is thrown at a time, the advancing with it is my own going forward. '

CHAP. XIX. The Master said, 'Never flagging when I set forth anything to him; — ah! That is Hûi.'

CHAP. XX. The Master said of Yen Yüan, 'Alas! I saw his constant advance. I never saw him stop in his progress.'

CHAP. XXI. The Master said, 'There are cases in which the blade springs, but the plant does not go on to flower! There are cases where it flowers, but no fruit is subsequently produced!'

CHAP. XXII. The Master said, 'A youth is to be regarded with respect. How do we know that his future will not be equal to our present? If he reach the age of forty or fifty, and has not made himself heard of, then indeed he will not be worth being regarded with respect.'

CHAP. XXIII. The Master said, 'Can men refuse to assent to the words of strict admonition? But it is reforming the conduct because of them which is valuable. Can men refuse to be pleased with words of gentle advice? But it is unfolding their aim which is valuable. If a man be pleased with these words, but does not unfold their aim, and assents to those, but does not reform his conduct, I can really do nothing with him.'

CHAP. XXIV. The Master said, 'Hold faithfulness and sincerity as first principles. Have no friends not equal to yourself. When you have faults; do not fear to abandon them.'

CHAP. XXV. The Master said, 'The commander of the forces of a large state may be carried off, but the will of even a common man cannot be taken from him.'

CHAP. XXVI. 1. The Master said, 'Dressed himself in a tattered robe quilted with hemp, yet standing by the side of men dressed in furs, and not ashamed; —ah! it is Yû who is equal to this.

2. '"He dislikes none, he courts nothing; —what can he do but what is good?"'

3. Tsze-lû kept continually repeating these words of the *Ode*, when the Master said, 'Those things are by no means sufficient to constitute perfect excellence.'

CHAP. XXVII. The Master said, 'When the year becomes cold, then we know how the pine and the cypress are the last to lose their leaves.'

CHAP. XXVIII. The Master said, 'The wise are free from perplexities; the virtuous from anxiety; and the bold from fear.'

CHAP. XXIX. The Master said, 'There are some with whom we may study in common, but we shall find them unable to go along with us to principles. Perhaps we may go on with them to principles, but we shall find them unable to get established in those along with us. Or if we may get so established along with them, we shall find them unable to weigh occurring events along with us.'

CHAP. XXX. 1. How the flowers of the aspen-plum flutter and turn! Do I not think of you? But your house is distant.

2. The Master said, 'It is the want of thought about it. How is it distant?'

BOOK X. HEANG TANG.

CHAPTER I. 1. Confucius, in his village, looked simple and sincere, and as if he were not able to speak.

2. When he was in the prince's ancestorial temple, or in the court, he spoke minutely on every point, but cautiously.

CHAP. II. 1. When he was waiting at court, in speaking with the officers of the lower grade, he spake freely, but in a straightforward manner; in speaking with the officers of the higher grade, he did so blandly but precisely.

2. When the ruler was present, his manner displayed respectful uneasiness; it was grave, but self-possessed.

CHAP. III. 1. When the prince called him to employ him in the reception of a visitor, his countenance appeared to change, and his legs to bend beneath him.

2. He inclined himself to the other officers among whom he stood, moving his left or right arm, as their position required, but keeping the skirts of his robe before and behind evenly adjusted.

3. He hastened forward, with his arms like the wings of a bird.

4. When the guest had retired, he would report to the prince, 'The visitor is not turning round any more.'

CHAP. IV. 1. When he entered the palace gate, he seemed to bend his body, as if it were not sufficient to admit him.

2. When he was standing, he did not occupy the middle of the gate-way; when he passed in or out, he did not tread upon the threshold.

3. When he was passing the vacant place of the prince, his countenance appeared to change, and his legs to bend under him, and his words came as if he hardly had breath to utter them.

4. He ascended the reception hall, holding up his robe with both his hands, and his body bent; holding in his breath also, as if he dared not breathe.

5. When he came out from the audience, as soon as he had descended one step, he began to relax his countenance, and had a satisfied look. When he had got to the bottom of the steps, he advanced rapidly to his place, with his arms like wings, and on occupying it, his manner still showed respectful uneasiness.

CHAP. V. 1. When he was carrying the sceptre of his ruler, he seemed to bend his body, as if he were not able to bear its weight. He did not hold it higher than the position of the hands in making a bow, nor lower than their position in giving anything to another. His countenance seemed to change, and look apprehensive, and he dragged his feet along as if they were held by something to the ground.

2. In presenting the presents with which he was charged, he wore a placid appearance.

3. At his private audience, he looked highly pleased.

CHAP. Ⅵ. 1. The superior man did not use a deep purple, or a puce color, in the ornaments of his dress.

2. Even in his undress, he did not wear anything of a red or reddish color.

3. In warm weather, he had a single garment either of coarse or fine texture, but he wore it displayed over an inner garment.

4. Over lamb's fur he wore a garment of black; over fawn's fur one of white; and over fox's fur one of yellow.

5. The fur robe of his undress was long, with the right sleeve short.

6. He required his sleeping dress to be half as long again as his body.

7. When staying at home, he used thick furs of the fox or the badger.

8. When he put off mourning, he wore all the appendages of the girdle.

9. His under-garment, except when it was required to be of the curtain shape, was made of silk cut narrow above and wide below.

10. He did not wear lamb's fur, or a black cap, on a visit of condolence.

11. On the first day of the month, he put on his court robes, and presented himself at court.

CHAP. Ⅶ. 1. When fasting, he thought it necessary to have his clothes brightly clean, and made of linen cloth.

2. When fasting, he thought it necessary to change his food, and also to change the place where he commonly sat in the apartment.

CHAP. Ⅷ. 1. He did not dislike to have his rice finely cleaned, nor to have his minced meat cut quite small.

2. He did not eat rice which had been injured by heat or damp and turned sour, nor fish or flesh which was gone. He did not eat what was discoloured, or what was of a bad flavour, nor anything which was not in season.

3. He did not eat meat which was not cut properly, nor what was served without its proper sauce.

4. Though there might be a large quantity of meat, he would not allow what he took to exceed the due proportion for the rice. It was only in wine that he laid down no limit for himself, but he did not allow himself to be confused by it.

5. He did not partake of wine and dried meat bought in the market.

6. He was never without ginger when he ate.

7. He did not eat much.

8. When he had been assisting at the prince's sacrifice, he did not keep the flesh which he received over night. The flesh of his family sacrifice he did not keep over three days. If kept over three days, people could not eat it.

9. When eating, he did not converse. When in bed, he did not speak.

10. Although his food might be coarse rice and vegetable soup, he would offer a little of it in sacrifice with a grave respectful air.

CHAP. Ⅸ. If his mat was not straight, he did not sit on it.

CHAP. Ⅹ. 1. When the villagers were drinking together, on those who carried staves going out, he went out immediately after.

2. When the villagers were going through their ceremonies to drive away pestilential influences, he put on his court robes and stood on the eastern steps.

CHAP. Ⅺ. 1. When he was sending complimentary inquiries to any one in another state, he bowed twice as he escorted the messenger away.

2. Chî K'ang having sent him a present of physic, he bowed and received it, saying, 'I do not know it. I dare not taste it. '

CHAP. Ⅻ. The stable being burned down, when he was at court, on his return he said, 'Has any man been hurt?' He did not ask about the horses.

CHAP. ⅩⅢ. 1. When the prince sent him a gift of cooked meat, he would adjust his mat, first taste it, and then give it away to others. When the prince sent him a gift of undressed meat, he would have it cooked, and offer it to the spirits of his ancestors. When the prince sent him a gift of a living animal, he would keep it alive.

2. When he was in attendance on the prince and joining in the entertainment, the prince only sacrificed. He first tasted everything.

3. When he was sick and the prince came to visit him, he had his head to the east, made his court robes be spread over him, and drew his girdle across them.

4. When the prince's order called him, without waiting for his carriage to be yoked, he went at once.

CHAP. ⅩⅣ. When he entered the ancestral temple of the state, he asked about everything.

CHAP. ⅩⅤ. 1. When any of his friends died, if he had no relations who could be depended upon for the necessary offices, he would say, 'I will bury him. '

2. When a friend sent him a present, though it might be a carriage and horses, he did not bow.

3. The only present for which he bowed was that of the flesh of sacrifice.

CHAP. XVI. 1. In bed, he did not lie like a corpse. At home, he did not put on any formal deportment.

2. When he saw any one in a mourning dress, though it might be an acquaintance, he would change countenance; when he saw any one wearing the cap of full dress, or a blind person, though he might be in his undress, he would salute them in a ceremonious manner.

3. To any person in mourning he bowed forward to the cross-bar of his carriage; he bowed in the same way to any one bearing the tables of population.

4. When he was at an entertainment where there was an abundance of provisions set before him, he would change countenance and rise up.

5. On a sudden clap of thunder, or a violent wind, he would change countenance.

CHAP. XVII. 1. When he was about to mount his carriage, he would stand straight, holding the cord.

2. When he was in the carriage, he did not turn his head quite round, he did not talk hastily, he did not point with his hands.

CHAP. XVIII. 1. Seeing the countenance, it instantly rises. It flies round, and by and by settles.

2. The Master said, 'There is the hen-pheasant on the hill bridge. At its season! At its season!' Tsze-lû made a motion to it. Thrice it smelt him and then rose.

后　记

笔者在 2011—2016 年在中山大学攻读博士学位期间，有幸加入黄国文老师指导的《论语》英译的研究团队，开始了对《论语》英译课题的研究。博士毕业后，笔者将研究所得运用于教学之中，给广东财经大学本科生开设了《论语》英译赏析的通识课程，受到学生们的欢迎。本书的出版，是对过去几年研究和探索《论语》英译赏析课程教学的一个总结。在教学过程中，笔者一直有一个心愿，就是让学生在阅读《论语》这部中国典籍代表作的时候，能够方便地阅读原文、理解原文，同时欣赏到不同译者的英文译文。因此，本书参考了杨伯峻、李泽厚、钱穆、天宜等学者的现代汉语译文，同时参考了理雅各、辜鸿铭、许渊冲、吴国珍等译者的英文译本。书中例句由《论语》原文、现代汉语译文（今译）、不同译者英译文（英译）、注释及讨论组成，方便读者充分理解原文，同时赏析不同译者对于同一原文的不同翻译方式。

本书的出版，离不开攻读博士学位期间打下的坚实基础，书中也参考了当时研究团队成员的部分研究成果，在此向导师黄国文教授、曾蕾教授及吴国向师兄表示衷心的感谢。

本书是在广东财经大学外国语学院院长陈冬纯教授和中山大学出版社熊锡源老师的竭诚帮助下面世的。感谢陈冬纯教授对本书出版的殷切关心和推动，感谢熊锡源老师在出版过程中的耐心指导和悉心帮助，感谢广东财经大学为本项目提供的资金支持。

胡红辉